# The Art Corner

**Bonnie Flint Striebel**
and
**Ruth Beazell Forgan**

**Goodyear Publishing Company, Inc.**
Santa Monica, California

Y-0641-4

ISBN:   0-87620-064-1

Current printing (last digit)
10   9   8   7   6   5   4   3

Printed in the United States of America

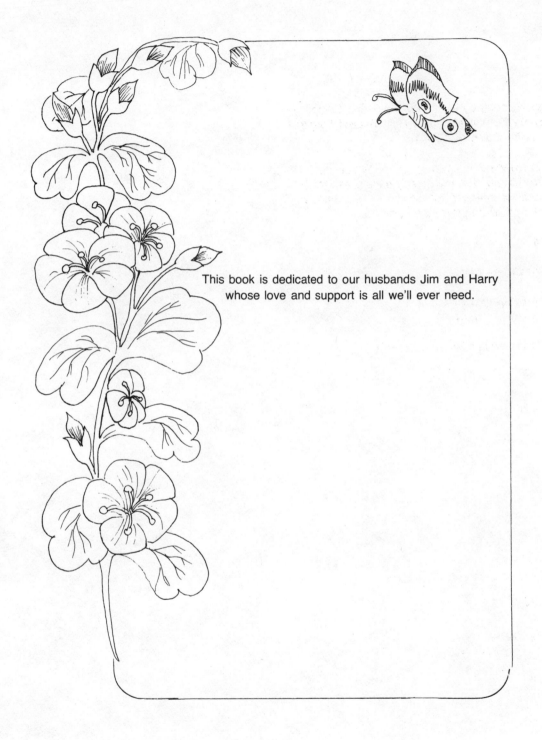

This book is dedicated to our husbands Jim and Harry
whose love and support is all we'll ever need.

# Contents

# Preface

When you ask elementary school children what their favorite subject is in school, many children will say art. Art is popular because it is fun—children like to do it. Yet in most elementary schools children are considered fortunate to have one hour of art instruction during the school week—a little over 30 hours of art from the 1,000 hours they spend in the classroom each year. Many teachers have set up an art corner or an art center as a way of providing additional activities for children to enjoy creating. This book is designed to provide teachers with the ideas and directions for providing more opportunities for art in the classroom. Thirty-six teacher-directed activities are included—one for each week of the school year. In addition, there are sixty independent activities which children can complete at the art corner. All of the activities include a title, description of the materials needed, time necessary to complete the project, and the directions for either the student or the teacher.

The activities designed for use by teachers with the total class require very little preparation. Materials used by the children are inexpensive and commonly available. Pictorial directions as well as brief written directions are provided, so it is not necessary for the teacher to spend many hours explaining projects to children. Likewise, the teacher need not be "an artist" to stimulate the talents and creative abilities of students, as the necessary patterns and outlines needed for the lessons are presented in a ready-to-duplicate fashion.

Sheets describing the activities to be completed independently by the students are also ready to use. The teacher can display these at the art center along with the materials that are needed. The students simply follow the pictorial directions or the written directions which are written simply.

The ideas in this book can be used in any elementary school program. From the beginning of September when children make name tags to display on their desk, to the end of the school year, when children make a collage with leftover materials in their desk, hours of excitement and pleasure will be derived. We hope you have as much fun with your students as we had with our children in developing this book.

We wish to thank Harry Forgan for helping us conceptualize and gently encouraging us to write this book. We deeply appreciate all of the help that he gave to us. We also want to thank our husbands, Jim and Harry, for their continuous encouragement, support, love, and understanding as they helped care for our children, overlooked messy homes, dirty laundry, and many telephone calls to each other. Their patience and belief in our work is very gratifying. Last, but not least, we wish to thank our children, Greg, Jimmy, and Jeff Striebel and Jennifer and Jimmy Forgan. They have helped us out greatly by field testing many of our ideas.

We would also like to take this opportunity to thank many friends who gave us helpful suggestions as we worked with different media, and to Maureen Kuiken who shared some of her teaching ideas with us.

# Introduction

Elementary school teachers have one of the most demanding vocations in the working world. They must be specialists in a variety of basic subjects: reading, mathematics, social studies, health, science, physical education, and yes, even art. And they must provide meaningful and enjoyable learning activities for more than one thousand hours during the school year. This book is designed to help you make many of those hours stimulating and exciting. *The Art Corner* provides ninety-six art activities which are presented in an easy-to-use format. Thirty-six of the activities are designed as teacher-directed activities. These are activities that require some demonstration and explanation for the students to complete successfully. The sixty additional activities are designed for independent use by students. They require very few materials and involve simple directions which do not need to be demonstrated by an adult. *The Art Corner,* then, provides the teacher and students with a smorgasbord of art activities from which they can select, salt, pepper, and garnish as desired using their own creative thoughts and designs.

This book was conceived one afternoon as we talked about our children. Our children love art activities, but only have art once a week even though there are idle moments in class when children want to do something other than "read a book." As former elementary school teachers and art teachers, we are aware of how much children like to create crafts or simply explore using different media. We've also had the satisfaction of seeing smiling faces say to us, "Look at mine!" As Scout leaders and Sunday school teachers, we know the frustration of trying to come up with creative ideas for crafts and projects at the last moment. We wrote this book, then, for teachers like us and for other adults who have shared some of our satisfactions and frustrations.

## USING THE TEACHER-DIRECTED ACTIVITIES

Four teacher-directed activities are provided for each month of the school year from September through June. It is possible for you to use one teacher-directed art activity per week with your students. The title of each activity, the materials you will need, time required including clean up, as well as the directions are indicated for each of the activities. In preparing to use the teacher-directed activities, you will want to pay particular attention to the materials required. In the Appendix we have included a ready-to-duplicate note to parents for materials that you may want to have children bring from home. For example, in September one of the activities is designed to help the children make an attractive pencil case. To make the pencil case, each child must have a paper towel tube. You can duplicate copies of the notes to parents and have a child cut these apart. Next have the children fill in the blanks describing what they need and the date it is needed. We have found that if you send these home in advance, more than likely you will end up with more materials than needed.

Most materials required for the teacher-directed activities are typically available in most elementary schools: construction paper, scissors, glue, crayons and markers, etc. We have suggested very few projects that require extensive preparation on the part of the teacher. Likewise, we have included teacher-directed projects which are possible with a class of thirty to thirty-five children. As you know, some art projects, such as using papier-mâché, are simply "too messy" for large groups of children.

As you prepare the art lesson, we suggest you actually make the project following the easy steps. This will help you demonstrate the directions for the students, and also motivate the students to complete the project. For example, when you are helping the children make leaf people during the month of September, you can actually gather together some leaves and twigs and make a leaf person. You can then direct the children to collect leaves and twigs and bring them into the classroom for the project. As you demonstrate the steps in making leaf people, you can emphasize the fact that not all people look the same; therefore, you do not expect the children to make a leaf person just like yours. In completing the leaf people project, you might also encourage the children to make a leaf person for each member of their family, including pets. *Always encourage the children to "do their own thing." This will foster creativity in completing the projects.* The major objective of this book is to have children experiment with different types of media, rather than just follow directions to come out with the pictured product.

If patterns are needed for any of the teacher directed activities, they will be found in the section "Patterns." The page number is indicated in the description of the materials. For example, if you are working with the children to make a Perky Peacock, the peacock pattern page is found on page 103 in the pattern section. We have included patterns for some of the projects because many children like to make something that is realistic. At the same time, we would encourage you to guide the children to be creative in using the patterns. Not all patterns must be colored or painted with the same colors or designs.

Sometimes it will be necessary for you to prepare some of the materials for use with the children. This is especially the case when recipes are needed to make bread dough or play dough. There is a separate section in the Appendix which includes recipes for

creating various art media. We have included more recipes than what you will need for projects in this book; however, the recipes are simple to prepare.

Encourage parents to save commonly discarded materials such as tinfoil, squeeze bottles, paper towel tubes, newspapers, magazines, fabric scraps, and yarn. Also, some parents may enjoy coming to the classroom to help the children during the art lessons. We realize it is difficult to give all the attention and direction to thirty children when there is only one of you! You might ask the parents of your students if any of them would like to help you during special art projects. Tell them that they need not be talented in art; just willing to give simple directions, praise children for their achievements, and provide the extra hands in preparing and distributing materials. You have our permission to duplicate copies of any of the teacher-directed activities that you may want to share with parents as they prepare to help you. Many parents will be willing to help since they always enjoy learning about new projects and enjoy "fun" activities with the children.

In addition to using the activities as they are organized month-by-month, you may want to correlate some activities with your content area subjects. For example, if you are studying about the presidents of the United States, you may want to use the activity involving Lincoln and Washington. This activity is designed for the month of February. However, you are encouraged to use any activity at the most appropriate times for your class. Likewise, many of the projects result in gifts for others. You might consider having the students make some of the Fold and Seal Stationery. The children can complete this project during their spare moments and enjoy working out their own designs. Then, as a class project or a spare time project, they can make the Treasure Box, which can be used for their Fold and Seal Stationery. We would encourage you to survey all of the activities listed in the Table of Contents so you can correlate some of them with other aspects of your school program.

As you use many of the teacher-directed activities, there will be opportunities to teach the children some aspects of art appreciation. For example, as the children complete the project on pointillism, you can tell them how pointillism started, and perhaps show them some pictures from the encyclopedia or other sources. Of course, as you demonstrate some of the steps in the teacher-directed activities, you can teach students ways of creating special effects with media. For example, when the children make the Hand Trees, you can show them how a pencil can be used to create special effects on construction paper.

A Lesson in Color and color wheel is provided in the Appendix. You are encouraged to duplicate a color wheel for each child and then have them complete their own color wheels to see how colors can be combined to form new colors. Even though this book is not designed to be a curriculum guide for art in the elementary school, you will find many opportunities to help children appreciate art and learn interesting techniques as they explore with different art media.

Some teachers do not teach art as frequently as they would like because children sometimes become too enthusiastic and cause many discipline problems. We are aware of the fact that children do look forward to art and enjoy a "good time" when they are working on art projects. In other words, during the art lessons you can expect more social interaction from the children, but at the same time, we share your concern about the safety and success of each child. We believe you will have better control of the children if you talk with them about the type of behavior you expect during the art period. Tell them that you know there will be more productive noise, but at the same time, you want to make sure there is no "tomfoolery" so no child will get hurt. For example, when children are using scissors, paint, and other art materials, there is the risk of someone getting hurt if certain rules are not followed. Tell the children you also enjoy the art activities and look forward to having fun with them. At the same time, you will want to make sure every child has a chance to create without being rudely interrupted by others, or threatened by sharp scissors or other materials. Tell the children that if rules are broken, those children who have broken the rules will

not be able to participate. Perhaps you would like to make rules such as the following:

Rules for Art Lessons
1. Listen to the teacher while she is talking.
2. Talk to others and share ideas as you complete your products.
3. Do not hurt anyone with materials or supplies.
4. Clean up your area and help put materials away.
5. Enjoy!

IF YOU CANNOT FOLLOW THESE RULES, YOU WILL NOT BE ABLE TO PARTICIPATE IN THE ART LESSONS.

## USING THE INDEPENDENT ACTIVITIES

The sixty independent activities provided in this book are those that most children can complete on their own without any assistance from an adult. The independent activities are presented in the same format as the teacher-directed activities. Children will read the title, list of materials that are necessary, the time required to complete the project, and pictorial step-by-step directions for completing the project. There are also some very simple written directions on the projects to clarify the illustrations. Your first step in using the independent activities is to read them and know which ones most of the children in your classroom can do independently. The activities are not organized according to grade level, but rather presented as a smorgasbord for you and your students. We have found that some second graders can do some of the projects that fifth graders cannot do. Some of the art activities are like good books—children want to do them again. Just as with good books, children get different things from the projects at different ages when they do them. As you read the independent projects, you can determine which ones are appropriate for your students or particular students within your class. If there are some activities that you feel your students cannot do independently, you might use these as additional teacher-directed projects.

The independent student activities are ready for you to use. You are encouraged to remove them from the book or make copies of them to be displayed at an art corner. You might remove the pages from the book and display two or four different activities each week. These could be placed in a manila folder for use by the children. If you desire, you do have our permission to make a thermofax master of the independent art activities, and provide a copy for each child. Many children will want to save the directions for the projects and do them again at home. As with the teacher-directed activities, children are encouraged to be creative. They may complete the same project several times, and end up with totally different products.

As you set up an art corner in your classroom, we encourage you to locate it near the sink, and away from centers in your classroom which involve quiet activities. The art corner should provide children an opportunity to make some productive noise and socialize as they work on their projects. Many times children will learn from each other as one child says to another, "Look at this!" Usually the question, "How did you do that?" follows and then the child becomes the teacher. You will need to talk with the children about the amount of noise you expect from the art corner as well as other rules for putting materials away and cleaning. We suggest making a list of these rules such as the following, and when they are not followed, close the art corner for awhile, or take away the privileges of using the art corner for students who are not following the guidelines. It won't be long until the art corner is open again, and the children are using it in an enjoyable and respectful manner.

### Rules for Using the Art Center
1. Talk quietly.
2. Put away all of the materials you get out.
3. Clean up your mess when you are done.
4. Display your project.
5. Place all discarded paper in the scrapbox.
6. Have fun!

REMEMBER, IF WE CANNOT USE THE ART CENTER WITHOUT DISTURBING OTHERS IN THE CLASSROOM, IT WILL BE CLOSED!

The basic materials you will need for an art corner are as follows: construction paper, scissors, glue, felt pens, crayons, scraps of paper, squeeze bottles, tempera paint, scraps of materials, wallpaper books that have been discarded, paper plates, yarn, coffee cans, paper towels, jars for water, pencils, and pens. Of course the materials that are needed for the various projects are outlined in the upper right-hand corner of each project, so it will be necessary for you to include only those materials which are needed for the projects you are displaying for the children. Please remember you can substitute materials for the different projects. For example, we have a section for newspaper projects, but this should not limit the possibilities of using newspapers and magazines in many of the projects throughout the book. Newspaper can be used for painting, backgrounds, crayon pictures, and so forth. Attach it to cardboard if it is too flimsy, make picture frames and flowers, gift wrap greeting cards, and collages. Be creative.

These materials might be located in the shelves or cabinets if they are available. If not, simply make an art corner by using cardboard boxes. You can encourage the children to bring cardboard boxes of varying sizes to class. By taping the boxes together, you can create a nice storage area for the materials at the art corner.

There may be some materials that you want the children to bring from home. Again, you can use the ready-to-reproduce notes describing particular projects. We have also included another ready-to-reproduce letter which you can use at the beginning of the year to encourage parents to save commonly discarded household materials. You might have the different members of your class be responsible for certain types of materials to make sure the art corner is well stocked. At the same time we would encourage you to talk with your children about not wasting materials. Some elementary school children

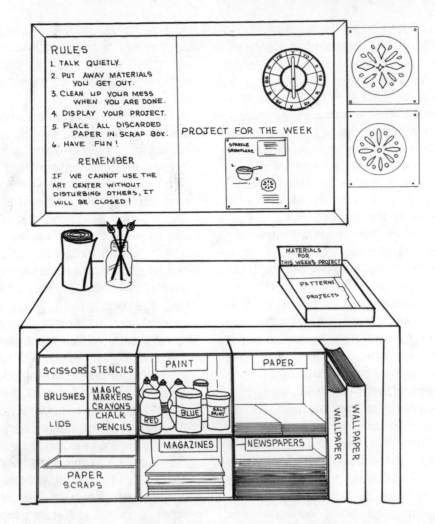

tend to begin a project, make something they don't want or make what they feel is a "mistake" and throw away the materials. Make sure you provide a scrapbox for pieces of construction paper, fabric, and other materials which can be used by the children. It is more important to have a scrapbox than it is to have a waste basket!

Since the independent activities will be completed by the students without your direction, you will need to provide some space in the classroom or display area where the children can show their projects to you and others. Make sure you take time to point out what you like about the projects as you nourish the creative talents of the children. The feedback you provide in terms of praise, smiles, and specific comments motivate the children.

There may be some children in the classroom who are particularly interested in art and are developing some talents in this area.

One of your responsibilities as a teacher is to nourish and foster this interest and the newly acquired talents. Perhaps you would like to duplicate some of the independent activities for children to do on their own on the weekends or during school vacations. Some of these children may be able to think of new activities which others in the class can do. Encourage these artistic children to make a list of the materials and directions for others to follow. Also have them display their product so others can see what to make. In other words, you can continue to add to the art activities in this book by using the talents of your children. This would be beneficial both to the children who are artistic, as well as those who desire additional ideas.

## USING THE PATTERNS
Some of the art projects for the teacher-directed and independent activities require patterns. These patterns are found in the

third section of this book. In addition, there are other patterns teachers frequently need. At the request of several teachers, we have included some commonly sought patterns which you can use for bulletin boards, displays, additional art projects, or in making games and activities in other areas of the curriculum. For example, if you desire to make a bulletin board for the month of January, you will find patterns of two children in snowsuits. They can be enlarged to be used on a bulletin board by making a transparency and using the overhead projector. You may want to provide the children with some of these patterns and encourage them to make bulletin board displays for window cases. They can combine their own work in addition to using some of the patterns.

In addition to the patterns, there is a poem for each month of the school year. These poems are specially designed to be incorporated into bulletin board displays. If the children make projects that you would like to display, or if you decide to make a bulletin board for each month, you are welcome to copy the poems to be used as a part of the bulletin boards. We tried to create poems which will be new to the children, and at the same time apply to seasonal activities.

## A SPECIAL WORD TO SCOUT LEADERS, SUNDAY SCHOOL TEACHERS, CAMP SUPERVISORS, PARENTS, AND OTHER ADULTS

Even though this book is designed especially for teachers, it is possible to use the ninety-six activities in other situations. As scout leaders and Sunday school teachers, we know that children enjoy having arts and crafts as a part of their meetings. All the activities in this book can be used by adults who are not certified teachers. Keep in mind that this book is for the non-artist teacher who wants to help children enjoy art and the products that can be created.

We suggest you make your art corner by taking a cardboard box and putting in it the materials and supplies that are needed in many of the activities. This will save last minute running around to find materials. If you go to an art supply store, we suggest buying the following materials for your art box: scissors, glue, crayons, felt pens, construction paper of various colors, tempera paint in several colors (at least primary colors), yarn, and 9″ × 18″ newsprint. The materials list is based on the assumption that you are responsible for arts and crafts for approximately 10 children. The art supplies are basic. You are encouraged to read the lists of materials for those activities you want to pursue to see if there are additional items you will need for some projects. Of course you are also welcome to use the ready-to-reproduce notes to parents which are available in the Appendix.

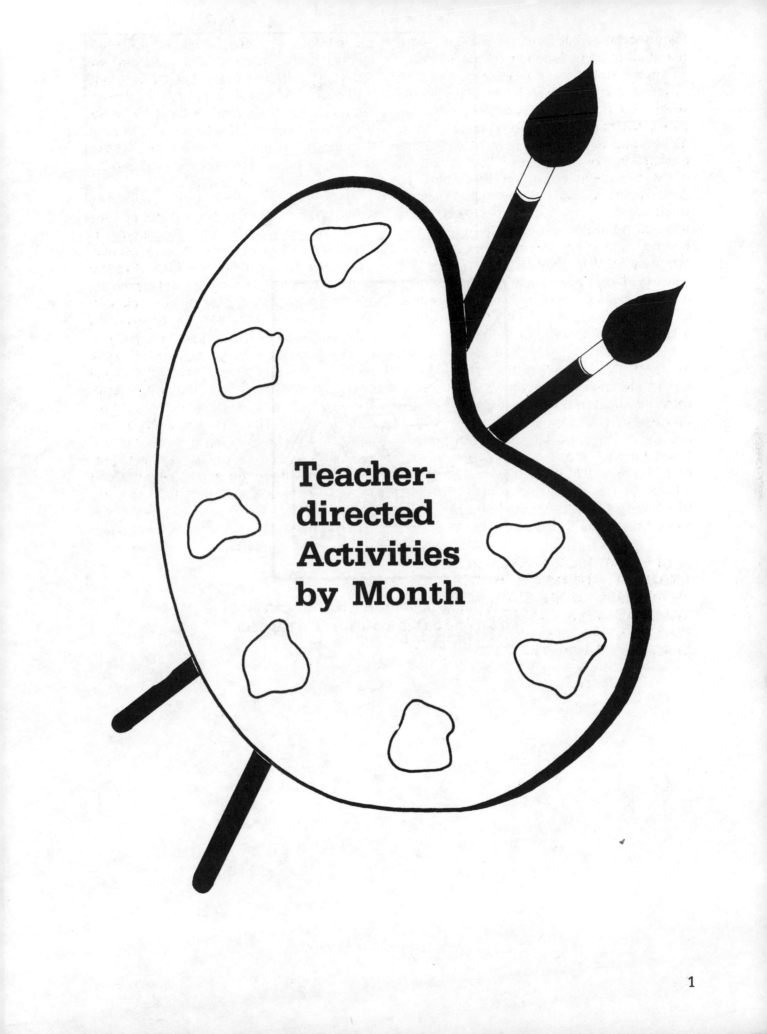

**Teacher-directed Activities by Month**

# First
# Day
# Desk
# Tags

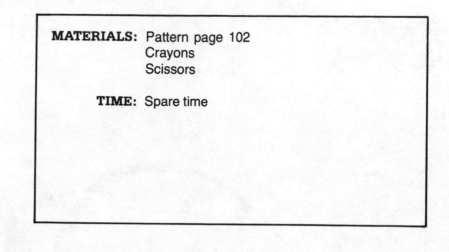

**MATERIALS:** Pattern page 102
Crayons
Scissors

**TIME:** Spare time

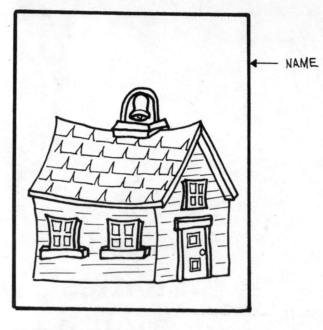

← NAME

Duplicate pattern. Each child can write his name on the top third of the paper and color the picture.

# Hand Tree

**MATERIALS:** 1 sheet of black construction paper
1 sheet of dark green construction paper
1 sheet of light green construction paper
½ sheet of brown construction paper
Scissors
Paste
Pencil

**TIME:** 45 minutes

**1.**

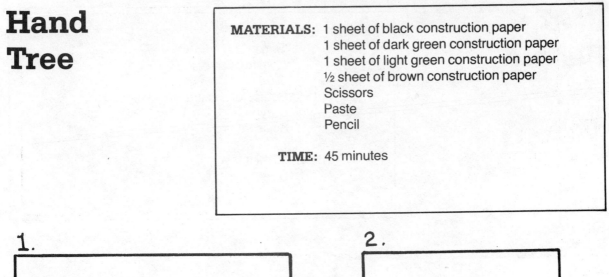

Spread fingers and trace hand on dark green and light green paper. This will make 4 to 6 hands. Cut them out.

**2.**

Tear a piece of brown paper for a tree trunk. Place on black paper. Do not glue.

**3.**

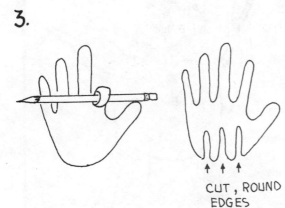

CUT, ROUND EDGES

Roll fingers and thumb of handprints over pencil to curl. On one hand cut 3 slits from bottom of palm to center. Round off edges and curl toward center. Use this for the center of the tree.

**4.**

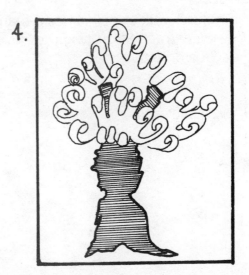

Paste 3 hands on tree. Glue on the trunk to black paper. Glue on center hand.

# Leaf
# People

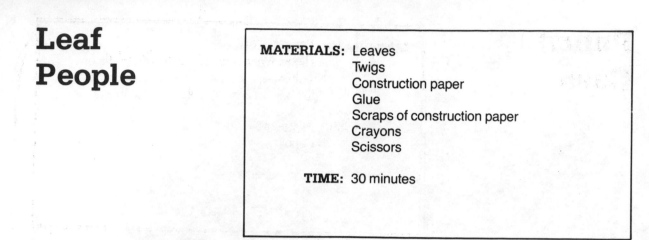

**MATERIALS:** Leaves
Twigs
Construction paper
Glue
Scraps of construction paper
Crayons
Scissors

**TIME:** 30 minutes

1.

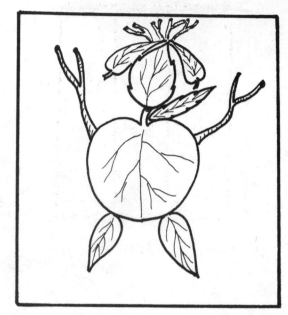

After a nature walk to collect leaves and small twigs, arrange the twigs to make people. Glue onto paper.

2.

Add other body parts using scrap paper and crayons.

# Pencil Case

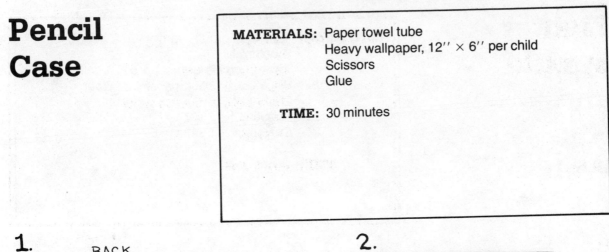

**MATERIALS:** Paper towel tube
Heavy wallpaper, 12″ × 6″ per child
Scissors
Glue

**TIME:** 30 minutes

**1.**

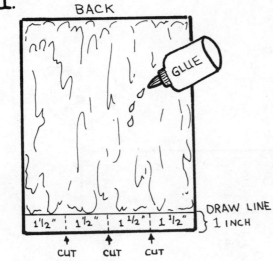

Spread glue to line.

**2.**

Wrap paper around the tube.

**3.**

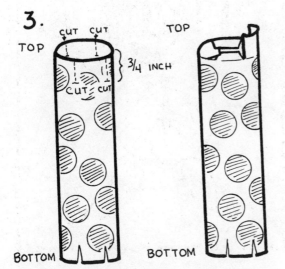

Cut top of cardboard into quarters. Fold in. Do not glue as this is the lid.

**4.**

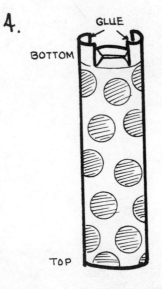

Fold bottom two flaps in. Glue two remaining flaps and press.

# Fighter Spider and His Web

MATERIALS: 4′ piece of orange yarn
8 toothpicks
Two 1″ circles of orange construction paper
Black construction paper for spider
Glue
Scissors
Crayon or felt pens

TIME: 1 hour

## 1.

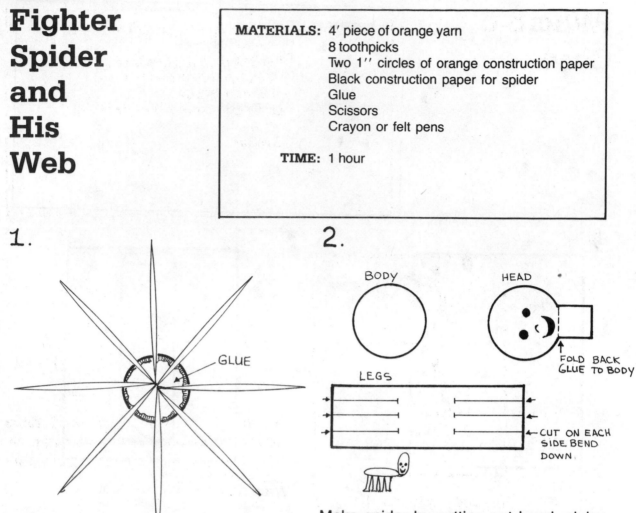

GLUE

Cover small circle with glue. Lay 8 toothpicks, touching in the center, on top of the glue. Spread glue on second circle and lay on top of toothpicks. Let dry.

## 2.

BODY

HEAD

FOLD BACK
GLUE TO BODY

LEGS

CUT ON EACH SIDE BEND DOWN.

Make spider by cutting out head, gluing neck to body, and gluing the legs onto the bottom.

## 3.

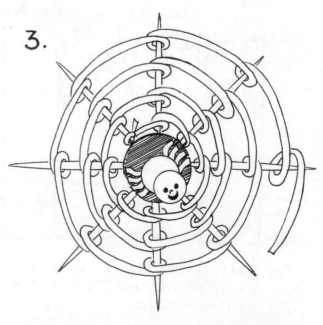

Weave Fighter Spider's Web with yarn. Tie a knot on a toothpick in the center. With yarn, loop over each of the toothpicks, leaving space between rows. When finished, tie knot. Glue Fighter Spider to the center.

# Who-o-o Owl

**MATERIALS:** Ten strips of ½'' × 12'' black construction paper
Small black scraps for eyes and beak
¼ page of yellow construction paper for moon and eyes
One sheet of orange construction paper
Glue
Scissors

**TIME:** 45 minutes

**1.**

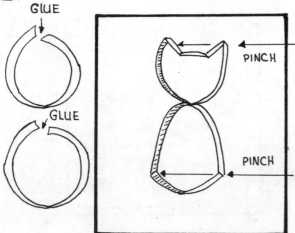

Glue circle for body and pinch. Glue slightly smaller circle for head and pinch. Glue each to paper.

**2.**

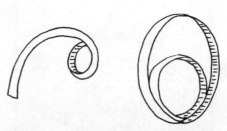

Cut one 12'' piece in half for eyes. Wrap around finger once and glue. Wrap remaining paper around again to form second circle. Repeat.

**3.**

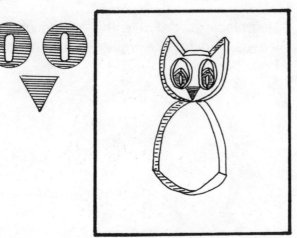

Cut 2 black circles and yellow centers to go under folded eyes and then glue. Cut triangle for beak and glue.

**4.**

Two or more strips may be glued for center of owl. Roll and pinch for design. Make branches and leaves. Add a yellow moon.

# Sort
# of
# Sumi

**MATERIALS:** Newsprint
Brush
Thin tempera—black and 2 colors
Pencil
Newspaper for under painting
Can of water

**TIME:** 1 hour

**1.**

Pencil lightly a simple line picture of leaves.

**2.**

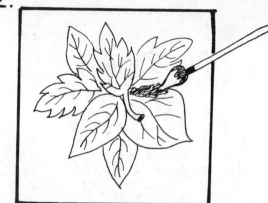

Load paint brush with paint and follow outside line of leaf. Paint will spread or run.

**3.**

Clean brush, use a new color. The spreading paint makes the picture have character.

**4.**

Use black for defining the outline of the leaves and for the veins in the leaves. Use sparingly.

# Creative Masks

**MATERIALS:** 1 sheet of construction paper
Scraps of construction paper
Scissors
Glue
String or yarn
Crayons

**TIME:** 30 minutes

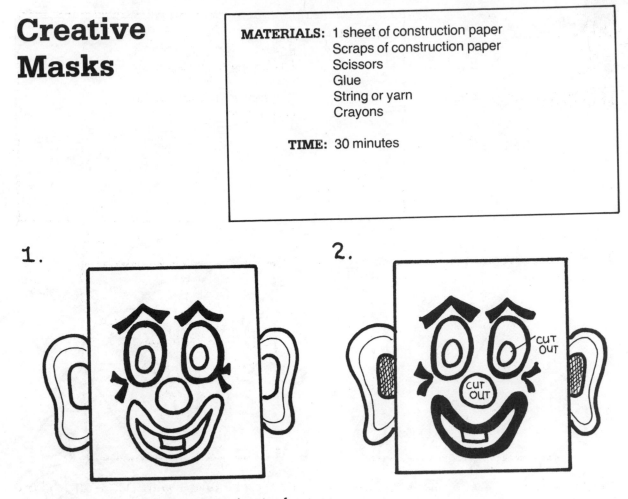

**1.**

Paste scraps of paper or color to form eyes, nose, mouth, and so forth.

**2.**

**3.**

Add hair, ears, hat, mustache, and so forth.

**4.**

Tie string on paper.

9

# Turkey Puppet

MATERIALS: Crayons
Pattern
Scissors

TIME: 30 minutes

CUT OUT

CUT OUT

Color turkey. Cut out. Insert fingers in holes to make turkey walk.

# Melt-A-Man

**MATERIALS:** Styrofoam cups
Crayons
Ink pen

**TIME:** 20 minutes

**1.**

Color a funny character head on the front and back of a cup.

**2.**

Outline around the eyes, mouth, and nose with an ink pen.

**3.**

Place cups on a cookie sheet, place rack in center of oven, and broil for 3 to 5 seconds.

**4.**

# Horn
# of
# Plenty

**MATERIALS:** Two sheets of 12″ × 18″ brown
      construction paper
      Stapler
      Glue
      Scissors
      Shredded newspaper
      Construction paper for fruit
      Crayons or felt pens

**TIME:** 30 minutes

1.

2.

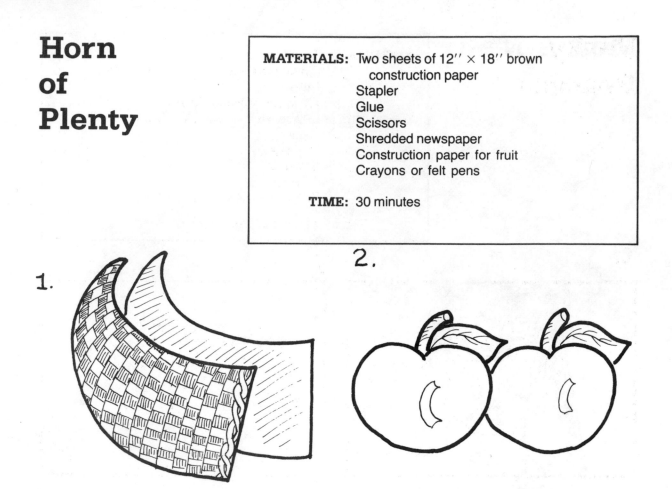

Cut 2 cornucopia from brown construction paper. Decorate outside if desired. Staple or glue together. Bend paper so it is round. Stuff crumpled newspaper into the tail to shape.

Have the children draw a fruit or vegetable on construction paper. Cut out and trace.

3.

4.

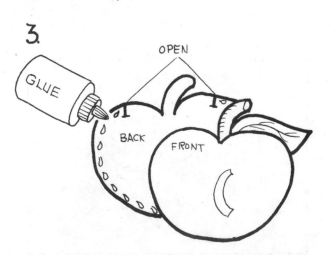

Place glue on back edge of one fruit or vegetable. Press together leaving an opening at the top.

Shred small amount of newspaper and carefully stuff to round out. Staple shut. Repeat with other fruits or vegetables to fill the cornucopia.

# Perky
# Peacock

**MATERIALS:** Tempera paint pad
(paper towel soaked in paint and folded)
Ruler
White construction paper
½ page each of two colors of construction
    paper
Crayons
Scissors
Glue
Peacock pattern page 103

**TIME:** 1 hour or more

**1.**

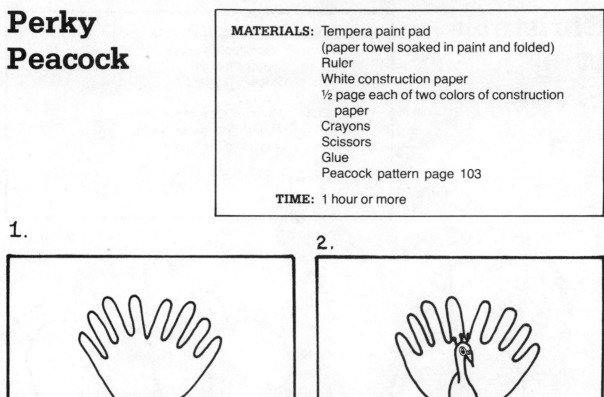

Lay hand, lifting up thumb, on paint pad. Stretch fingers wide and press onto construction paper. Repeat, overlapping palms. If you desire you may trace around hand and omit paint pad.

**2.**

If paint was not used, color hands. Color Peacock pattern and cut out. Glue pattern onto lower part of handprints. Draw legs.

**3.**

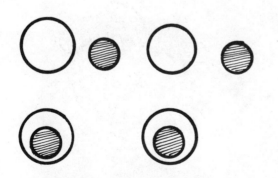

Cut out 18 large circles (about ¾″) and 18 smaller circles (about ½″). Glue together.

**4.**

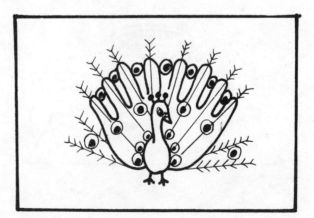

Using crayons and a ruler draw lines through fingers to the bird. Draw feather marks. Glue circles on bird.

# Christmas Wreath

**MATERIALS:** Wire coat hanger
Crepe paper strips—2″ × 6″
Styrofoam cups
Tinfoil

**TIME:** 1 hour

**1.**

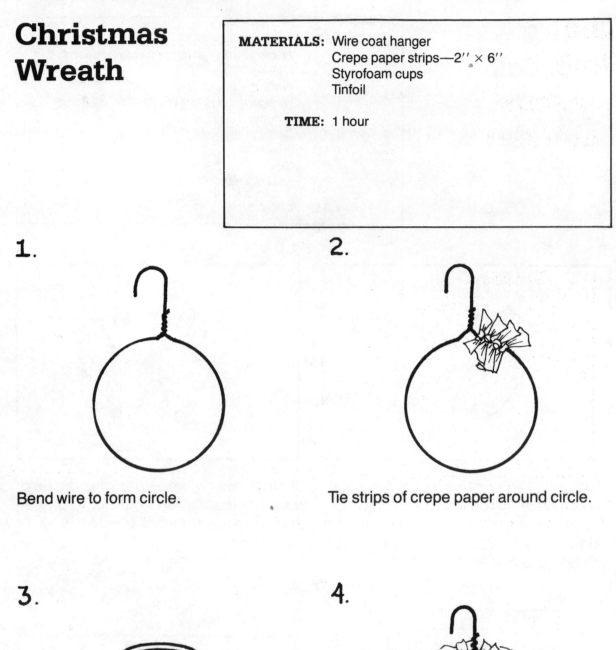

Bend wire to form circle.

**2.**

Tie strips of crepe paper around circle.

**3.**

Cover 2 cups with tinfoil. Poke a hole with pencil in bottom of cup.

**4.**

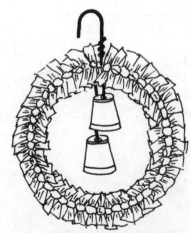

Stretch crepe paper strip and twist. Put into cup and tie knot. Repeat. Tie both to hanger.

# The Four Seasons Calendar

**MATERIALS:** Six calendar sheets, see pattern page 104
1 sheet of construction paper
Stapler
Ruler
Pencil
Crayons

**TIME:** Spare time project.

**1.**

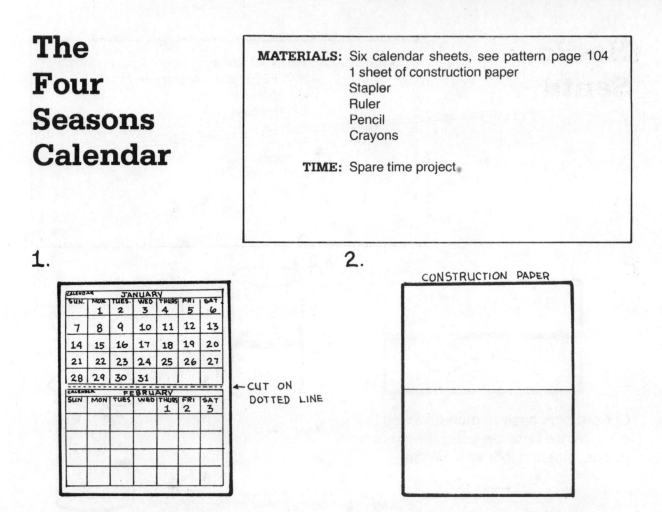

Label months and days on calendars. Cut calendar pages in half.

**2.**

Measure and draw a line across the center of construction paper.

**3.**

Measure and divide top half of paper into quarters. Label seasons and decorate.

**4.**

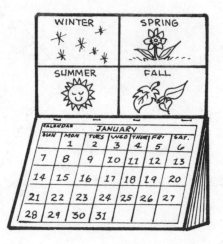

Staple the calendar pages to the lower half.

15

# Ho-Ho Santa

**MATERIALS:**  1 sheet of red construction paper cut in half
9'' × ¾'' strip of black paper
Scrap of pink paper
3 cotton balls
Pattern
Glue
Scissors
Red crayon
Stapler

**TIME:**  45 minutes

**1.**

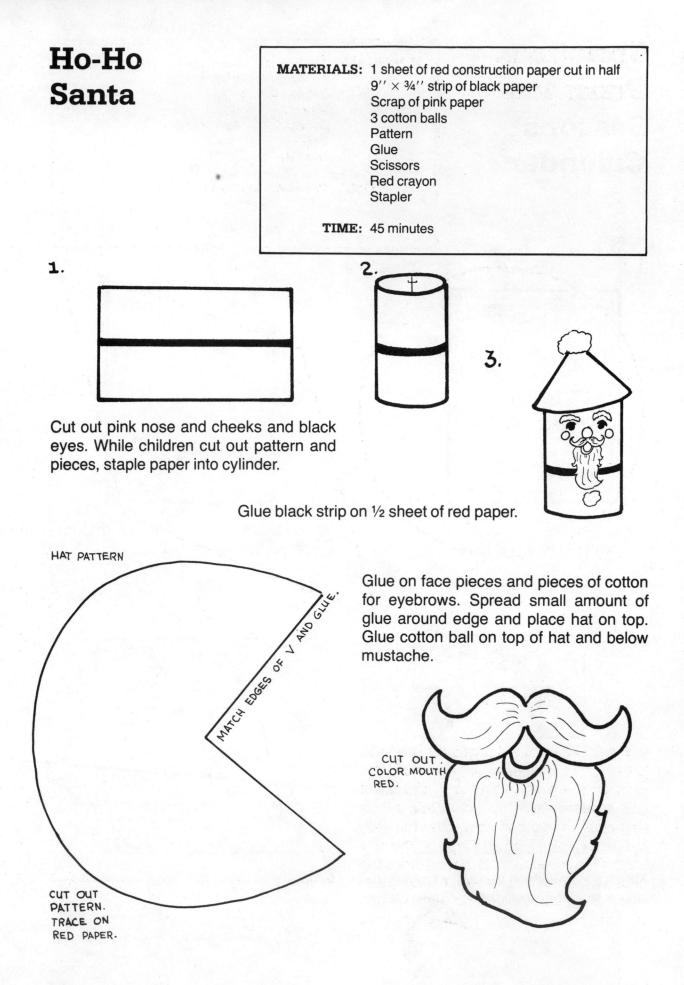

Cut out pink nose and cheeks and black eyes. While children cut out pattern and pieces, staple paper into cylinder.

**2.**

Glue black strip on ½ sheet of red paper.

**3.**

HAT PATTERN

MATCH EDGES OF V AND GLUE.

CUT OUT PATTERN. TRACE ON RED PAPER.

Glue on face pieces and pieces of cotton for eyebrows. Spread small amount of glue around edge and place hat on top. Glue cotton ball on top of hat and below mustache.

CUT OUT. COLOR MOUTH RED.

# Christmas Ornament

**MATERIALS:** Paper or felt
12″ piece of yarn or ribbon
Beads, sequins, glitter
Stickers
Cutouts from Christmas wrap
Glue
Scissors

**TIME:** 45 minutes to 1 hour

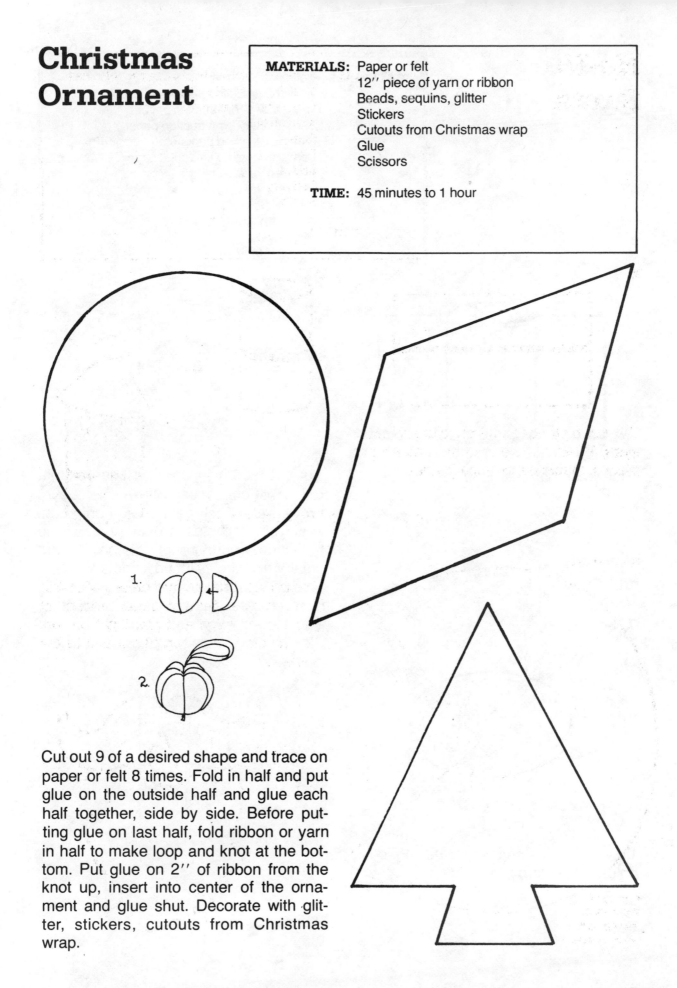

1.

2.

Cut out 9 of a desired shape and trace on paper or felt 8 times. Fold in half and put glue on the outside half and glue each half together, side by side. Before putting glue on last half, fold ribbon or yarn in half to make loop and knot at the bottom. Put glue on 2″ of ribbon from the knot up, insert into center of the ornament and glue shut. Decorate with glitter, stickers, cutouts from Christmas wrap.

17

# Clown
# Catch-all

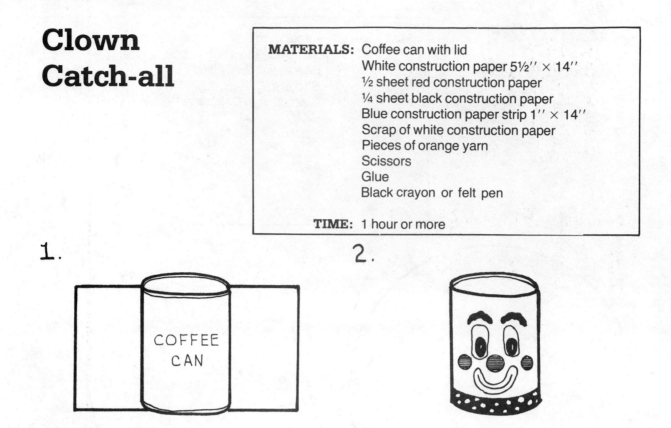

**MATERIALS:** Coffee can with lid
White construction paper 5½″ × 14″
½ sheet red construction paper
¼ sheet black construction paper
Blue construction paper strip 1″ × 14″
Scrap of white construction paper
Pieces of orange yarn
Scissors
Glue
Black crayon or felt pen

**TIME:** 1 hour or more

**1.**

Glue white paper around can.

**2.**

Cut out mouth, nose, and cheeks from red construction paper; eyes and eyebrows from black paper. Glue onto can. Draw black circles around eyes. Glue blue strip around bottom of can. Cut out small white circles for polka dots and glue onto blue paper.

**3.**

Tie yarn pieces onto lid for hair. Place lid on can. Trim yarn if desired.

**4.**

18

# Little Benny

**MATERIALS:** White paper pattern (see page 105)
2″ × 9″ colored construction paper
4″ × 2″ construction paper base
Scrap of construction paper for hands of
   clock
Brad
Glue
Scissors

**TIME:** 1 hour

**1.**

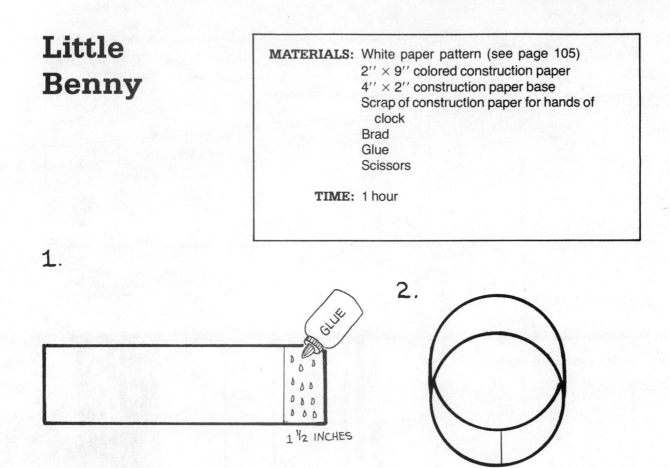

1 ½ INCHES

Measure 1½ inches and draw line.
Spread glue to line.

**2.**

Make circle, matching end of paper to
line on other end.

**3.**

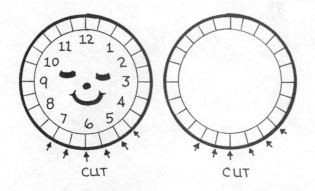

CUT        CUT

Cut out pattern pieces. Trace hands on
colored construction paper, cut out. Attach hands on face of clock with a brad
to form the nose.

**4.**

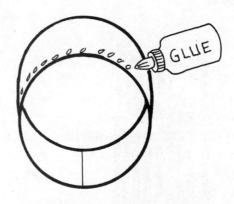

GLUE

Drip a thin line of glue on outside edge of
circle. Spread with finger, and attach
face. Repeat for back. Glue to a 4″ × 2″
base.

# Pom-Pom

MATERIALS: 2″ × 2″ cardboard square
9 yards or more of yarn
Scissors

TIME: 20–30 minutes

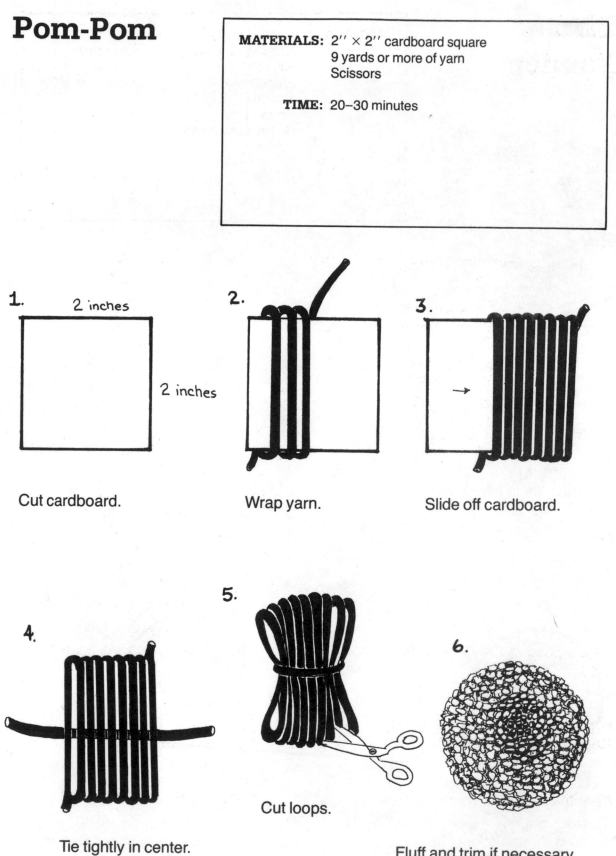

**1.** 2 inches / 2 inches

Cut cardboard.

**2.** Wrap yarn.

**3.** Slide off cardboard.

**4.** Tie tightly in center.

**5.** Cut loops.

**6.** Fluff and trim if necessary.

# Bird
# Feeder

**MATERIALS:** 1 styrofoam cup
2 foot piece of string
Scissors
Ballpoint pen
Crayons
Pencil
Bird seed or crumbs

**TIME:** 30 minutes

**1.**

Draw a design on the cup with ballpoint pen. Color with crayons.

**2.**

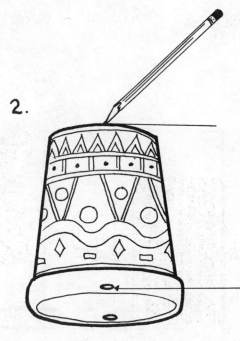

Poke a small drainage hole in the bottom of cup with a pencil.

Poke holes on each side of cup and tie string.

Fill with bread crumbs or seeds.

21

# Lincoln
# or
# Washington
# Silhouette

**MATERIALS:** 1 red weaving sheet pattern page 106
1 white weaving strip pattern page 107
1 blue silhouette pattern page 108 or 109
Glue
Scissors

**TIME:** 1 hour

**1.**

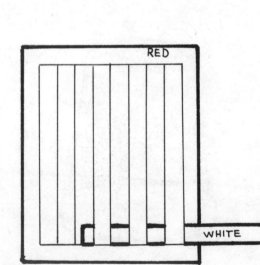

Carefully cut pattern of Lincoln or Washington. Discard center.

**2.**

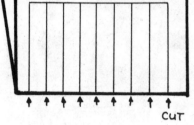

Fold red construction paper pattern in half, with lines outside. Children should cut to parallel line.

**3.**

Have children cut out white strips and weave into red paper.

**4.**

Glue silhouette frame over weaving.

22

# Valentine Straw Collage

**MATERIALS:** Different lengths of cut straws
Jar of half water and half glue
Wet paper towel for hands
Scissors
½ sheet red construction paper
Glue
2 paper plates
*Cotton fabric square—11″ × 11″
2″ brush

**TIME:** 1 hour or longer

\*TEACHER:
You may want to precut circles of fabric because children may find it difficult to do with school scissors.

**1.**

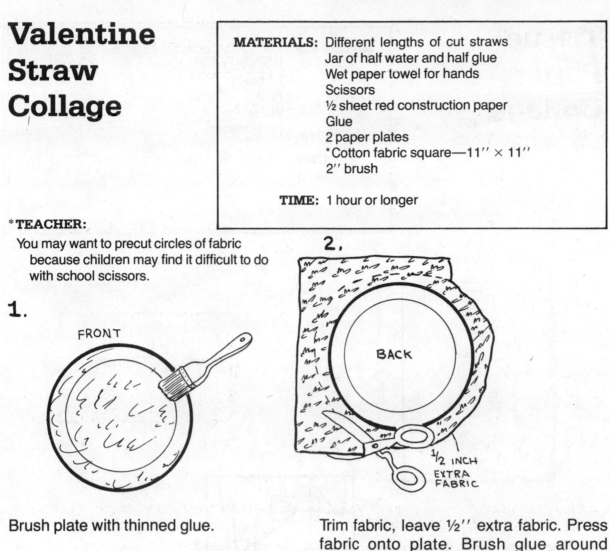

Brush plate with thinned glue.

Trim fabric, leave ½″ extra fabric. Press fabric onto plate. Brush glue around back rim of plate and press ½″ extra fabric under. Brush thinned glue on second plate. Lay plate 1 onto plate 2 and press edges.

**3.**

Cut 1 large heart out of red paper. Glue to fabric plate using regular glue. Cut out smaller hearts to decorate edge of plate.

**4.**

Dip ends of straws in glue. Stand upright in a double row around edge of large heart.

# Tissue
# Paper
# Collage

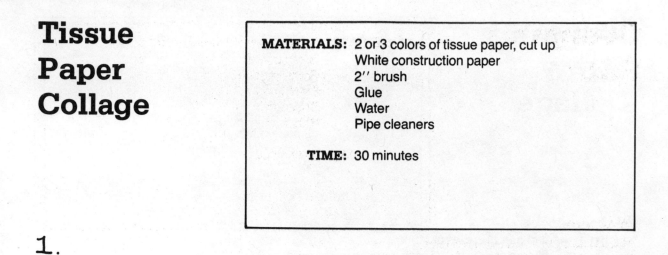

**MATERIALS:** 2 or 3 colors of tissue paper, cut up
White construction paper
2″ brush
Glue
Water
Pipe cleaners

**TIME:** 30 minutes

**1.**

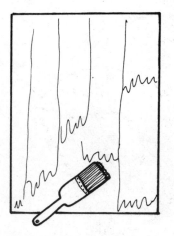

Mix glue with water, half and half.
Brush on white construction paper.

**2.**

Lay tissue paper on glue and cover page.

Let dry.

Spray with acrylic if you want it to be shiny.

**3.**

Glue pipe cleaners in a flower design.

# George's Hat

MATERIALS: * Blue construction paper 12″ × 18″
Scrap of red
Scrap of green
Black crayon
Scissors
Glue

TIME: 30 minutes

* **TEACHER:**
You will need to make the hat pattern.
The outside circle is 12″. The inside circle is
6″.

**1.**

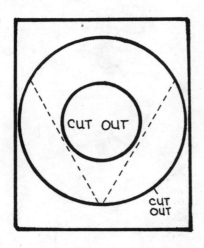

**2.**

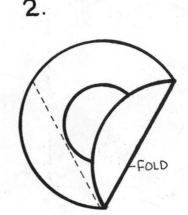

**3.**

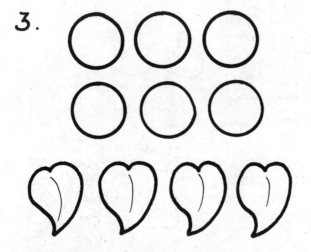

**4.**

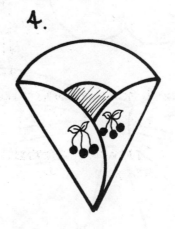

Have children cut out 6 small circles for cherries. Cut out 4 green leaves.

Glue 3 circles on each flap. Use black crayon to make stems. Glue leaves onto stems.

# Shamrock Family

**MATERIALS:** Green construction paper
Two strips 1″ × 12″ black construction
paper
Scissors
Glue
Pictures of family members

**TIME:** 30 minutes

1.

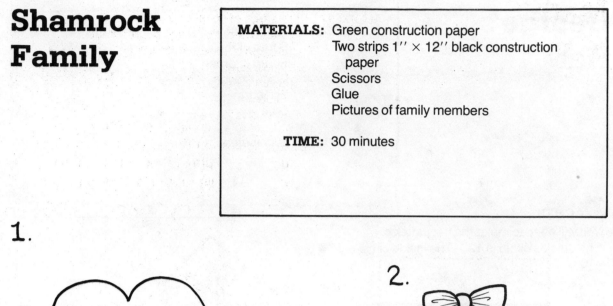

Cut out patterns and trace on green paper.

2.

Glue black strips together. Glue shamrocks and bow to black strip. Put a family member's picture in the center of each shamrock.

# Math Kite

**MATERIALS:** 1 sheet of construction paper
1 strip of construction paper for tail
Scraps of construction paper
Bow pattern
Scissors
Glue
Crayons

**TIME:** 20 minutes

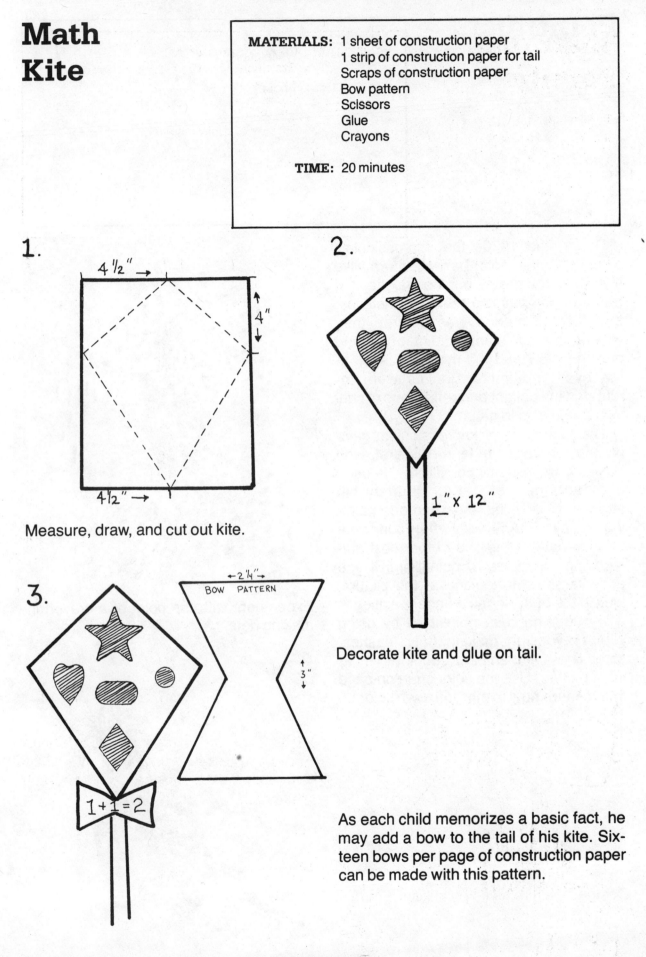

**1.**

Measure, draw, and cut out kite.

**2.**

Decorate kite and glue on tail.

**3.**

As each child memorizes a basic fact, he may add a bow to the tail of his kite. Sixteen bows per page of construction paper can be made with this pattern.

# Pointillism

**MATERIALS:** Crayons
White paper

**TIME:** 1 hour

During the 1870s the impressionists discovered that color became more alive if it was not mixed on the palette, but rather on the painting itself. For instance, if the color orange was desired they would put a dot, smear, or line of red and one of yellow and the mixing was left to the eye. The impressionists were interested in sunlight and reflections of sunlight on objects in nature.

The technique of impressionism gave way to the style of George Seurat, who invented the style of pointillism. He used dots and dashes rather than brush strokes. One of his most famous paintings is called, "A Sunday Afternoon on La Grande Jatte." It is one of the most outstanding examples of pointillism. If you are interested in looking at the picture, look in the encyclopedia under painting.

Try your hand at pointillism by using your crayons in making dots, dashes, small lines, and smears of color in making a picture. Use the color chart on page 141 to learn how to mix your own colors.

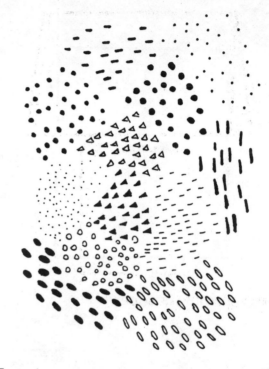

Experiment with the point of a crayon in making dots.

Design a picture using pointillism.

# Picture Frame

**MATERIALS:** 1 sheet of construction paper
Scissors
Pencil
Glue

**TIME:** 15 minutes

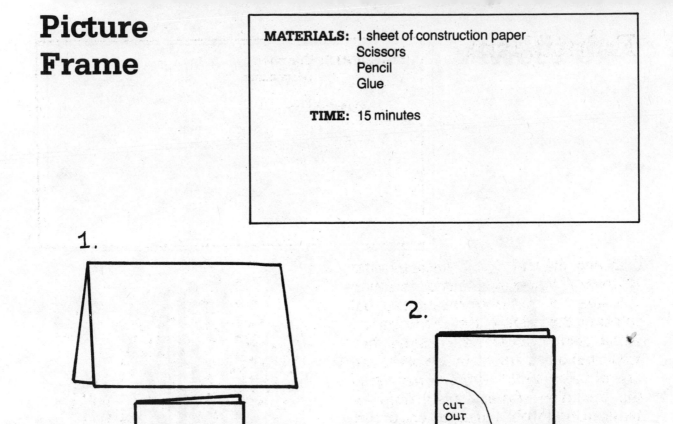

1.

Fold paper into quarters.

2.

CUT OUT

CUT

3.

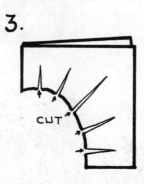

CUT

4.

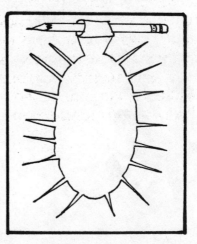

Roll each section around a pencil to curl.
Glue frame onto picture.

29

# Yarn Flower

**MATERIALS:** Three 38″ pieces of colored yarn
Green yarn for stems, leaves, and grass
Three 3″ pieces of another color yarn for center
1″ × 1½″ piece of cardboard
½ piece of construction paper
Glue
Scissors
Hair spray or acrylic spray

**TIME:** 45 minutes

**1.**

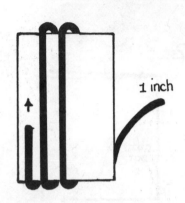

Wrap the long piece of yarn around length of cardboard. Leave 1″ of yarn at beginning and end.

Carefully slip yarn off cardboard and tie in center with short piece of yarn.

**2.**

Tie yarn in the back after wrapping.

**3.**

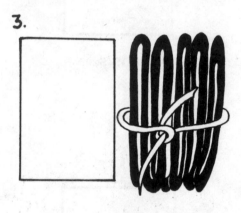

**4.**

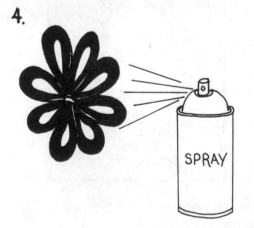

Spread loops and spray to stiffen.

**5.**

Make 2 more flowers and glue them to construction paper. Use green yarn for stems, leaves, and grass.

# Easter Bonnet Contest

**MATERIALS:** Newspaper   Glue
Yarn   Scissors
String   Balloons
Construction paper scraps
Ribbons and bows
Fabric scraps
Felt pens
Crayons
Stapler

**TIME:** 1 hour

1.

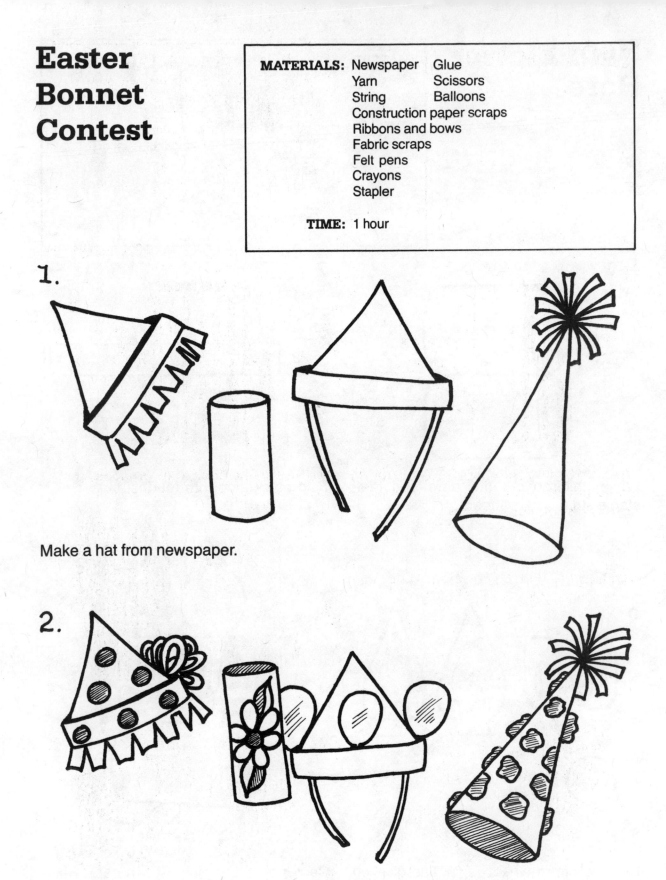

Make a hat from newspaper.

2.

Decorate with anything you want.

# Hoppy Hare

**MATERIALS:** Happy Hare pattern, page 110
1 sheet of blue or yellow construction paper
¼ sheet of pink paper
½'' × 9'' strip of black paper
Scrap of white paper
Glue
Scissors
Stapler
Cotton Ball

**TIME:** 45 minutes

**1.**

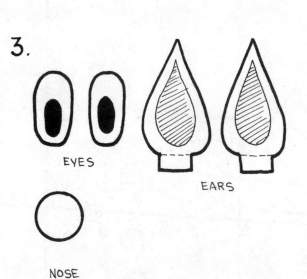

While children cut out ears and feet, staple strips into cylinders.

**2.**

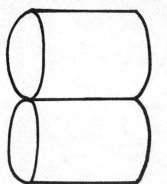

Fold black strip into fourths, cut.

**3.**

Cut eyes from white paper and glue on pupils. Cut out pink nose. Cut out pink lining for ears and glue onto ears.

**4.**

Center feet and glue. Attach ears, whiskers, nose, and cotton ball for tail.

# Arbor Day

**MATERIALS:** 1 sheet white construction paper
Brown tempera paint in squeeze bottle
Green tempera paint in jar lid
Yellow tempera paint in jar lid
Small sponge pieces about 1″ × 1″
Straw

**TIME:** 30 minutes

## 1.

Squeeze about 1 teaspoon of brown paint on white construction paper.

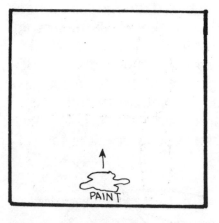

## 2.

Point end of straw at paint and blow in the direction you want the paint to move. Form trunk and branches. Add more paint if necessary. Let dry.

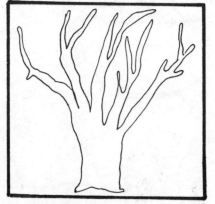

## 3.

Use a separate sponge for the yellow paint and one for the green paint. Sponge the leaves over and around the branches.

# Mother's Day Gift

**MATERIALS:** Driftwood, bark, wood, masonite or any
natural material at least 5" × 7"
Bread dough, see recipe page 136
Pieces of thinly sliced green sponge
Straw flowers or dried weeds
Cement glue

**TIME:** 2-day project—1 hour per day

Make bread dough day ahead. Have children make small mushrooms, birds, butterflies, and so forth. Each child should make 3 or 4 objects. Bake bread dough according to directions and seal. Place on natural material and glue on mushrooms and flowers. Apply sponge last for ground or grass to add color.

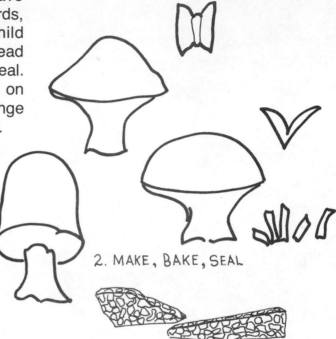

2. MAKE, BAKE, SEAL

1. MIX

3. CUT THIN PIECES OF SPONGE

4. GLUE

34

# May
# Day
# Baskets

MATERIALS: One paper plate
Stapler
Crayons or paint
Scissors
Paint brush
Scraps of construction paper
1″ × 10″ strip of construction paper for
handle

TIME: 30 minutes

## 1.

Cut paper plate in half. Each child will
have 2 half plates and a handle.

## 2.

Make a design on one side of each plate
half using crayon, paint or construction
paper.

## 3.

Fold into cup shape and staple together
at the top. Staple on handle.

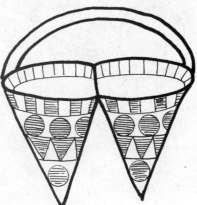

# Egg
# Shell
# Container

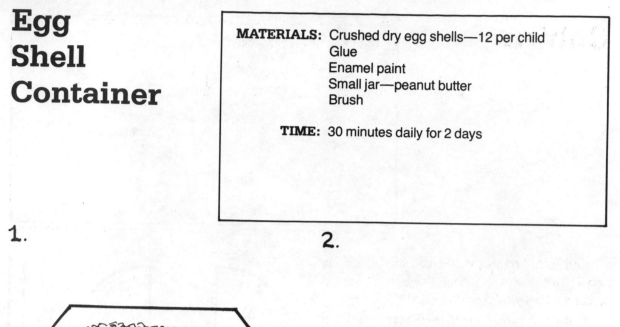

**MATERIALS:** Crushed dry egg shells—12 per child
Glue
Enamel paint
Small jar—peanut butter
Brush

**TIME:** 30 minutes daily for 2 days

1.

Lay egg shells on waxed paper.

2.

Cover jar with glue.

3.

Roll in crushed egg shells until completely covered. Allow to dry for a day.

4.

Paint with enamel paint. Dry. Use for planter, vase, or pencil holder.

# Cubism

MATERIALS: Crayons
Pencil
Ruler
Construction paper

TIME: 1 hour

Cubism developed in the early 1900s, and the effect could be seen in major works of art through the 1950s.

Pablo Picasso and Georges Braque were two famous painters who led this movement. To find out more about cubism, look in the encyclopedia under painting, cubism, Braque, and Picasso. There will be several examples of cubism.

The idea behind cubism is to take a familiar subject such as a table and break it down into shapes such as rectangles and triangles. Then flatten them and change the shape and color. After you break the object down the object is reassembled. The result is a new shape or form that barely resembles the original subject.

Decide what you want to draw and try to organize it as a cubist would have, using squares, rectangle patterns and odd shapes to draw your picture. Use crayons to color your picture.

THE TIRED KNIGHT

Independent
Student
Activities
by Media

# Merry Mobiles

**MATERIALS:** Beads from "Bread Dough Beads" (see page 44)
String or yarn
Popsicle sticks

**TIME:** 30 minutes

1.

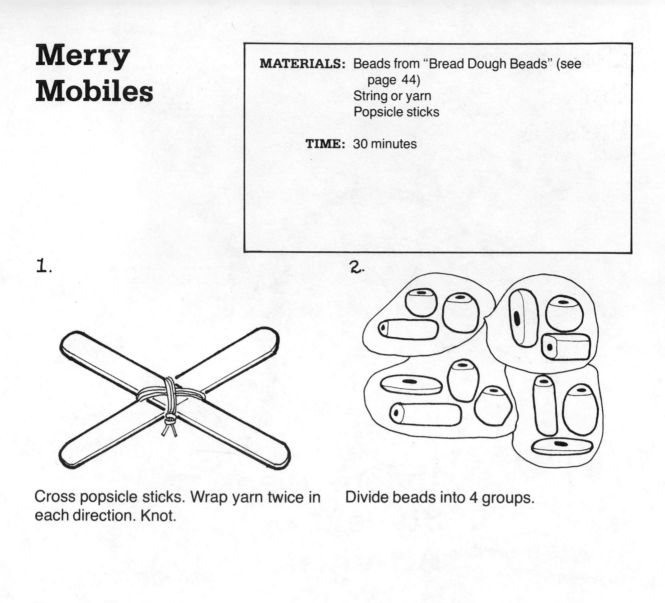

Cross popsicle sticks. Wrap yarn twice in each direction. Knot.

2.

Divide beads into 4 groups.

3.

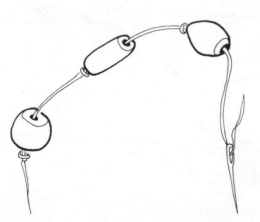

String beads on 4 strings. Leave 4″ at the top of each string.

4.

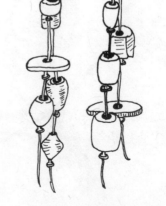

Tie 1 string of beads to each end of popsicle stick.

# Classroom Pet Parade

**MATERIALS:** Branch attached to bulletin board or a branch in a can of sand
¼ sheet of white construction paper
Paper punch
Yarn
Scissors
Crayons

**TIME:** 30 minutes

**1.**

Draw a picture of your pet.

**2.**

Cut out pet and color on both sides.

FRONT

**3.**

Write your pet's name and your name. Punch a hole, tie on yarn and hang on branch.

BACK

YOUR NAME
PETS NAME

*From* The Art Corner © *1979 Goodyear Publishing Company, Inc., Bonnie Flint Striebel, and Ruth Beazell Forgan*

# Cupid Mobile

**MATERIALS:** 1 wire hanger
Cupid pattern page 111 on red construction paper
Small piece of string
1 sheet of red construction paper
Glue
Scissors

**TIME:** 30 minutes

1.

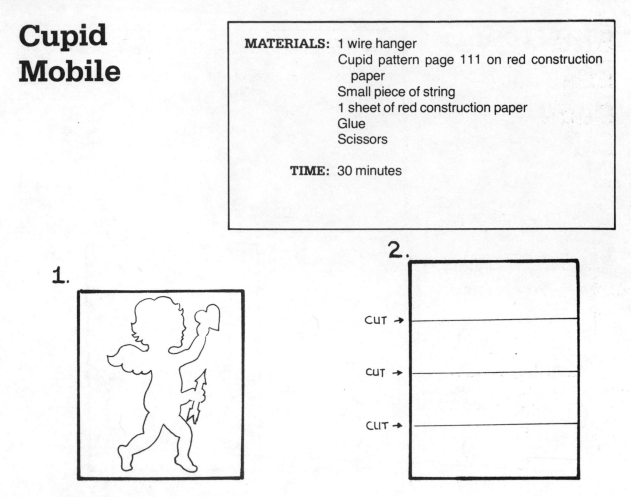

Cut out cupid pattern.

3.

Fold and cut out hearts. Trace on remaining paper and cut.

4.

Bend hanger. Hang cupid and glue hearts back to back on hanger.

# Bird
# in a
# Cage

**MATERIALS:** 4″ × 9″ piece of construction paper
Ruler
Scissors
Bird pattern, page 112
Yarn or string
Crayons

**TIME:** 1 hour or more

**1.**

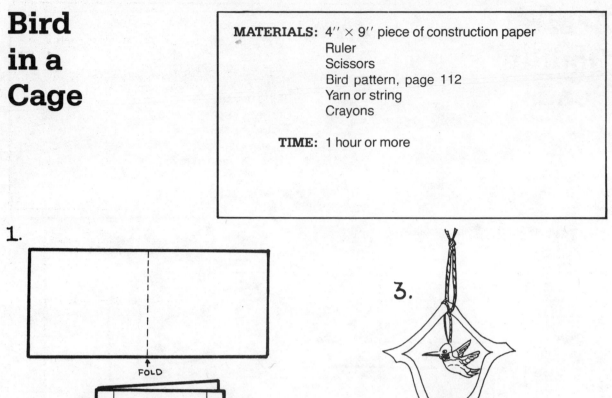

FOLD

Draw a line 1″ from edge on each end. Divide space between into four 1″ sections.

**2.**

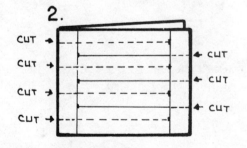

CUT
CUT
CUT
CUT
CUT
CUT
CUT
CUT

Divide each 1″ section in half. Draw a line from 1″ vertical line to edge. Repeat, alternating edges. Cut through both layers from the edge where arrow points to the vertical line. Open carefully and stretch.

**3.**

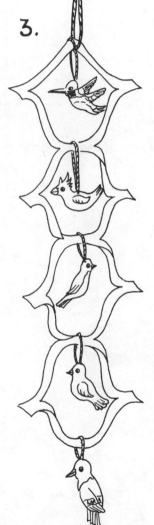

Color birds on both sides and cut out. Hang in the center of each section with yarn or string.

# Bread
# Dough
# Beads

**MATERIALS:** * Bread dough recipe—doubled (see page 136)
Covered container for bread dough
Toothpicks
String or yarn
Shellac or spray acrylic
Tempera paint—optional
Brush—optional
7″ × 12″ strip of tinfoil

**TIME:** 20–30 minutes daily for 4 days

* May be used for jewelry or mobiles. See page 40.

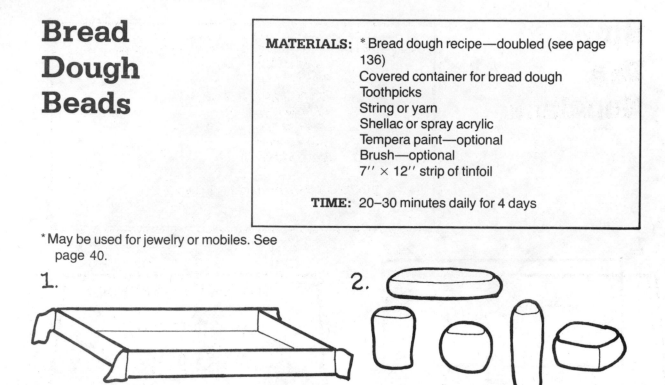

**1.**

Fold sides up on tinfoil. Pinch the corners to make a box. Write name very carefully in a corner with pencil. Use box to hold your beads.

**2.**

Make different shape beads.

**3.**

Using a toothpick poke a hole through the center of each bead.

**4.**

Your teacher will bake these. Then you may paint them. Let dry.

**5.**

Spray beads two times with shellac. Let dry between each spray.

**6.**

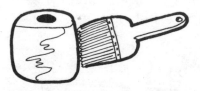
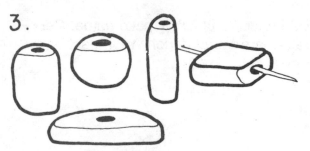

String your beads. Tie a knot between each bead.

From The Art Corner © 1979 Goodyear Publishing Company, Inc., Bonnie Flint Striebel, and Ruth Beazell Forgan

# Name
# Tag
# Necklace

**MATERIALS:** Colored salt flour dough (see recipe
page 138)
Pencil
Round object, such as jar lid
30'' piece of yarn
Dark felt pen
Spray acrylic
Square of tinfoil

**TIME:** 15 minutes daily for 2 days

**1.**

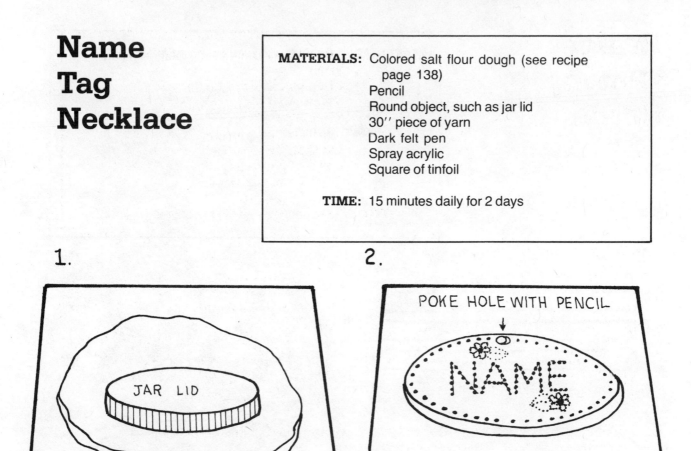

Pat dough ¼'' thick on tinfoil. Use jar lid
and cut a circle.

**2.**

POKE HOLE WITH PENCIL

Use pencil and lightly poke name. Decorate the edge of dough. Your teacher will
bake your name tag.

**3.**

When dry use felt pen and trace your
name and design. Spray both sides with
acrylic. Dry, spray again.

**4.**

Tie yarn through the hole. Wear the name
tag around your neck.

# Finger
# Pot

**MATERIALS:** Bread dough (see recipe page 136)
Newspapers
Pencil
Water in jar lid

**TIME:** 30 minutes

**1.**

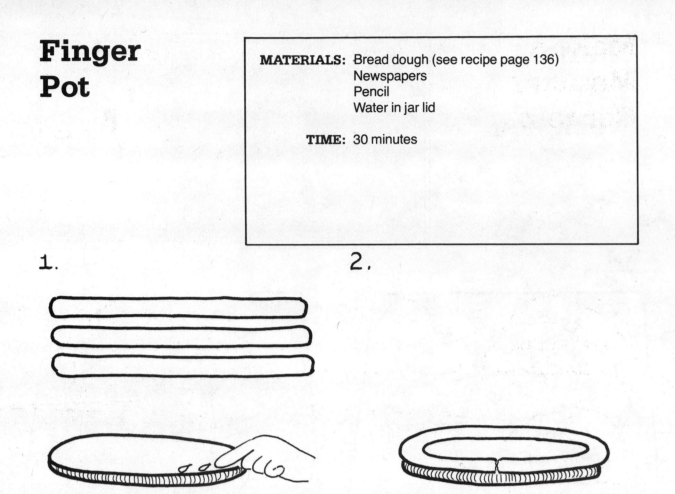

Roll dough into strips. Make circle for bottom. Dab water around the edge of circle.

**2.**

Lay strip on the circle and pinch off the extra.

**3.**

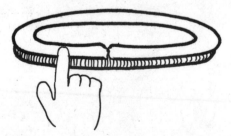

Lightly press layers together with finger to make the outside smooth. Dab water around the top. Repeat steps 2 and 3 until finished.

**4.**

Use a pencil to make designs on the outside. Let dry for several days.

# Make a Monster Contest

**MATERIALS:** Play dough in 4 colors (see recipe on page 136)
Pencil
Newspapers

**TIME:** 30 minutes

1.

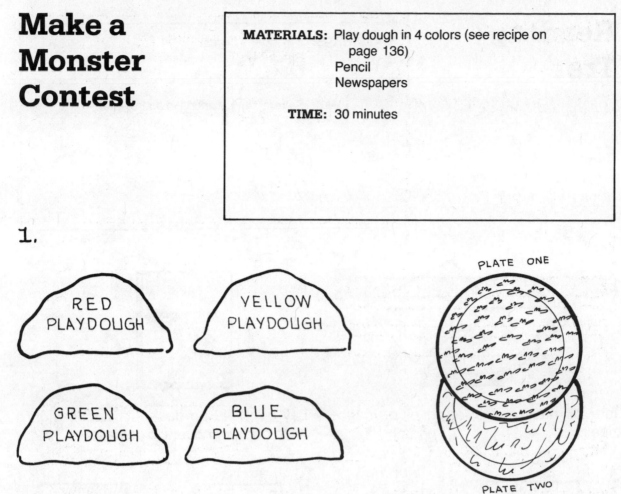

RED PLAYDOUGH

YELLOW PLAYDOUGH

GREEN PLAYDOUGH

BLUE PLAYDOUGH

PLATE ONE

PLATE TWO

2.

Roll strips, make squares, circles, and balls. Use your pencil to make textures. Make the ugliest monster and win the contest.

*From* **The Art Corner** © *1979 Goodyear Publishing Company, Inc., Bonnie Flint Striebel, and Ruth Beazell Forgan*

# Reading Tree

**MATERIALS:** 1 Reader's Digest
Spray paint
Construction paper

**TIME:** Several days working in spare time.

**1.**

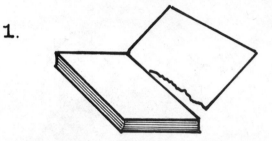

Tear off back and front cover of magazine.

**2.**

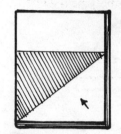

Lay book flat on desk. Lift bottom right-hand corner and fold to center.

**3.**

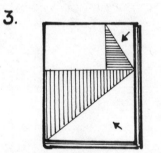

Lift top righthand corner and fold to meet edge of first fold.

**4.**

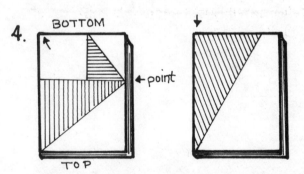

Now lift point and fold to the bottom edge, matching the straight sides.

**5.**

Do this for every page. Stand up and you have a tree.

**6.**

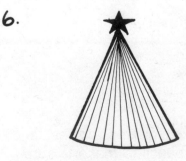

Spray tree any color. Cut out star and put on top. Decorate.

*From The Art Corner © 1979 Goodyear Publishing Company, Inc., Bonnie Flint Striebel, and Ruth Beazell Forgan*

# Money Pot

**MATERIALS:** *Magazines
Empty salt box
Glue
Scissors
Wet paper towel for fingers
Spray acrylic—optional

**TIME:** Spare time project

*__TEACHER:__ Depending on grade level, you may have to
cut magazine into 5″ × 5″ strips.

1.

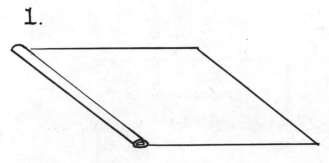

Make small folds, then roll a 5″ × 5″
strip of magazine.

2.

Glue edge and hold for a moment. Make
30–35 rolls.

3.

Glue rolls to the salt box.

4.

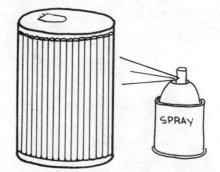

Spray acrylic if you would like.

*From* The Art Corner © 1979 *Goodyear Publishing Company, Inc., Bonnie Flint Striebel, and
Ruth Beazell Forgan*

# School Play Wig

**MATERIALS:** *18 magazine strips 1″ × 11″
Several magazine pages
Glue or stapler
2 bobby pins

**TIME:** 2 hours

**\* TEACHER:**
If you want to use glue instead of a stapler you can use full sheet of magazine. Start with step 2.

**1.**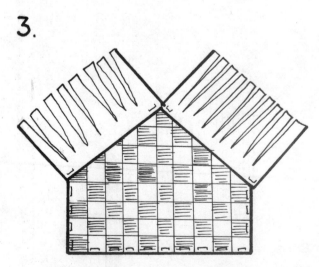

Weave strips and staple or glue on each end.

**2.**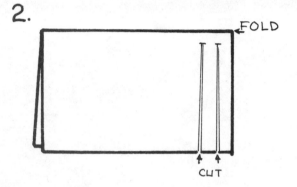

Fold magazine pages in half. Cut strips across page almost to the fold.

**3.**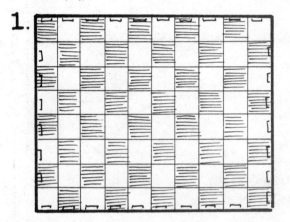

Staple around edges of woven magazine page. Continue stapling to the center, overlapping the pages so the wig will be bushy.

**4.**

Crumple the shredded strips so they stick up. Attach to hair with 2 bobby pins.

# Alphabet
# Magazine
# Montage

**MATERIALS:** Magazine
9″ × 12″ piece of construction paper
Scissors
Glue

**TIME:** 1 hour

## 1.

Cut two large letters from a magazine. Use your initials.

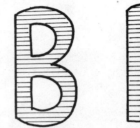

## 2.

Glue letters in the center of the page.

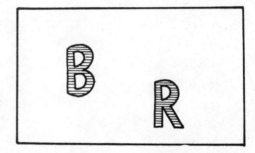

## 3.

Cut out letters of the alphabet from A to Z. Glue around the large letters. Decorate your reading corner.

# Initial
# Design

**MATERIALS:** 3 colors of paint
Brush
Paper
Pencil

**TIME:** 1 hour

## 1.

Draw initial on paper.

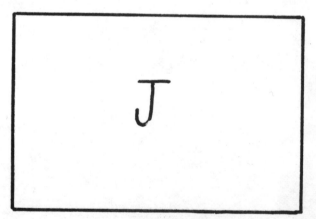

## 2.

Paint over initial.

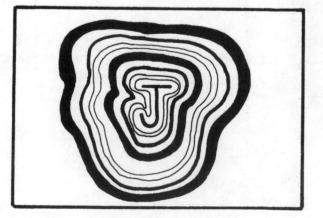

## 3.

Outline in different colors. Make some lines heavy and some thin.

*From* The Art Corner © *1979 Goodyear Publishing Company, Inc., Bonnie Flint Striebel, and Ruth Beazell Forgan*

# Blotto
# Creatures

**MATERIALS:** Construction paper
2 colors of tempera in squeeze bottles
Crayons or felt pens
2 jar lids
Paint brush

**TIME:** 30 minutes

**1.**

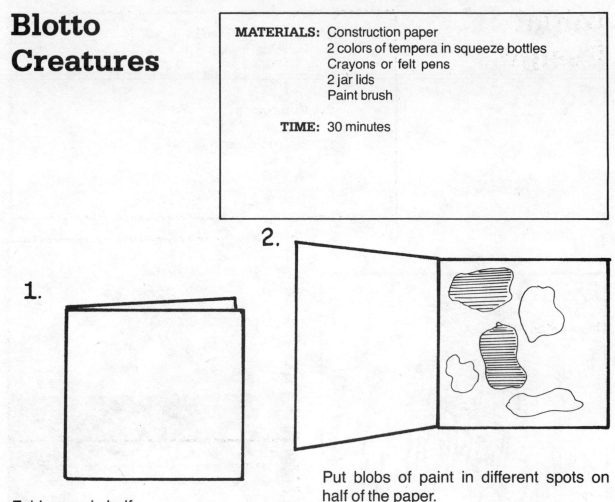

Fold paper in half.

**2.**

Put blobs of paint in different spots on half of the paper.

**3.**

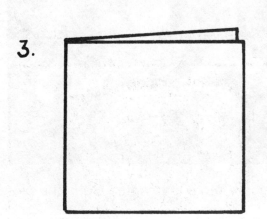

Fold paper over and rub.

**4.**

Open, let dry. Outline creatures and make faces on each. Cut in half. Keep one and display one.

# Sugar
# Chalk
# Clown

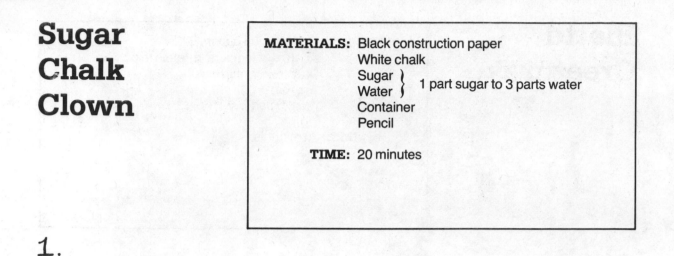

**MATERIALS:** Black construction paper
White chalk
Sugar ⎫
Water ⎬ 1 part sugar to 3 parts water
Container
Pencil

**TIME:** 20 minutes

## 1.

Pencil sketch drawing on paper.

## 2.

Dip chalk into sugar water. Color the picture.

*From The Art Corner* © *1979 Goodyear Publishing Company, Inc., Bonnie Flint Striebel, and Ruth Beazell Forgan*

# Sparkle Snowflake

**MATERIALS:** Salt paint recipe, page 137
Brush
Construction paper
Scissors
Use construction paper snowflake, page 67

**TIME:** 20 minutes

1.

Make salt paint mixture.

2.

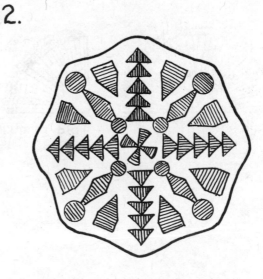

Have children cut out snowflakes. Brush one side of snowflake lightly with salt paint. Let dry. Brush second side and let dry. Display.

# Cupcake
# Collage

**MATERIALS:** 12 baking cups
½ sheet black construction paper
Glue

**TIME:** 15 minutes

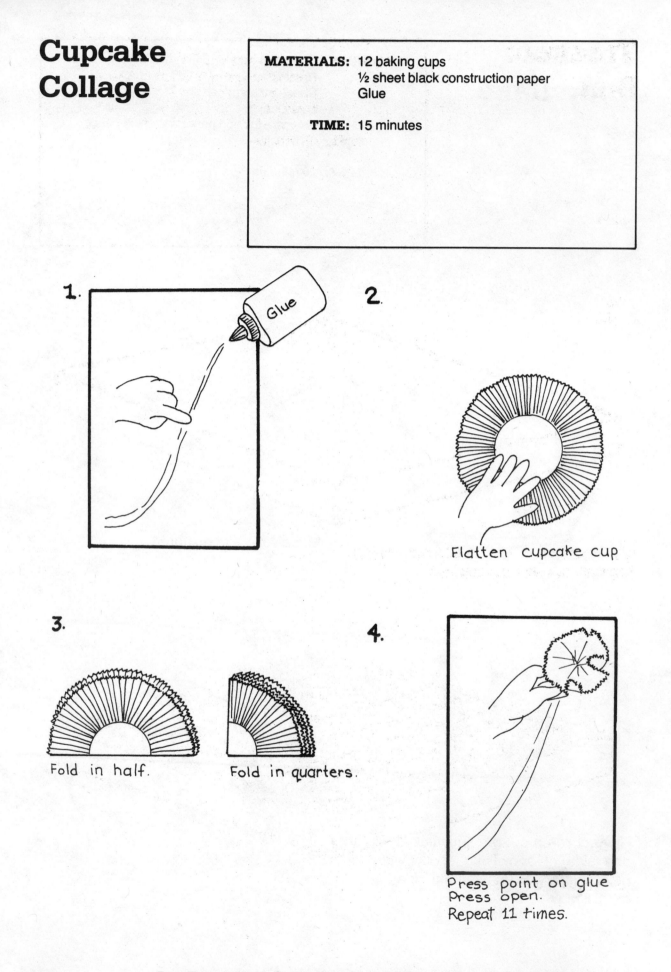

1.

2.

Flatten cupcake cup

3.

Fold in half.    Fold in quarters.

4.

Press point on glue
Press open.
Repeat 11 times.

*From The Art Corner © 1979 Goodyear Publishing Company, Inc., Bonnie Flint Striebel, and
Ruth Beazell Forgan*

# Treasure Box

**MATERIALS:** Stationery size box
Seashell macaroni or other type macaroni
Lid for glue
Spray paint

**TIME:** 45 minutes

1.

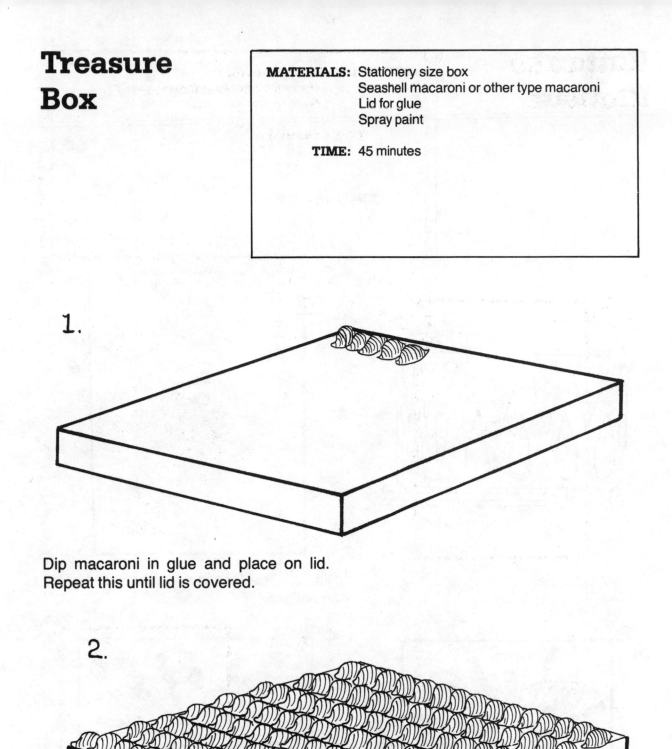

Dip macaroni in glue and place on lid.
Repeat this until lid is covered.

2.

Let dry and spray paint.

# Button
# Flower

**MATERIALS:** 1 sheet of construction paper
Scraps of colored construction paper
Scraps of green construction paper
Glue
Scissors
Buttons
Yarn for stem

**TIME:** 30 minutes

1.

Cut out large petal shapes.

2.

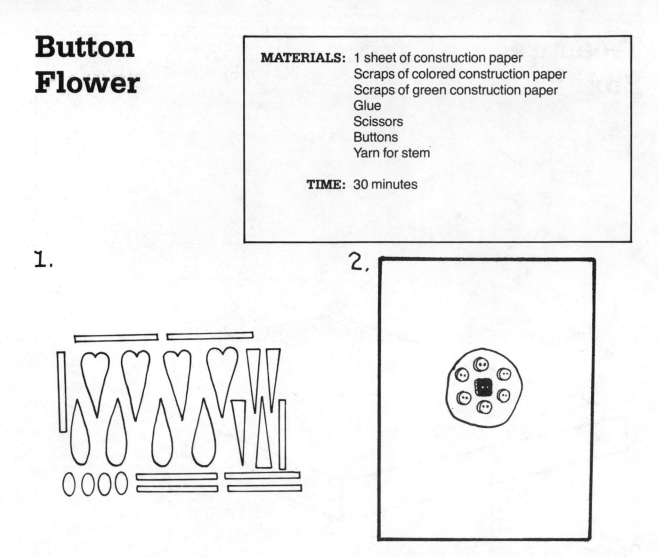

Cut out circle for center of flower and glue on buttons.

3.

Glue petals around the center.

4.

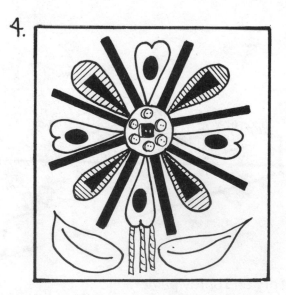

Cut strips of yarn for stems and glue on leaves.

*From The Art Corner* © *1979 Goodyear Publishing Company, Inc., Bonnie Flint Striebel, and Ruth Beazell Forgan*

# End of the Year Collage

MATERIALS: Anything in your desk you can glue on
paper and would be throwing away
Heavy tagboard
Glue

TIME: 1 hour

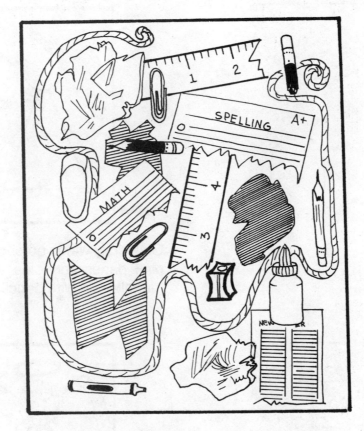

Arrange the material you have found on
your paper to form an interesting design.
Glue down.

# Heavenly Angel

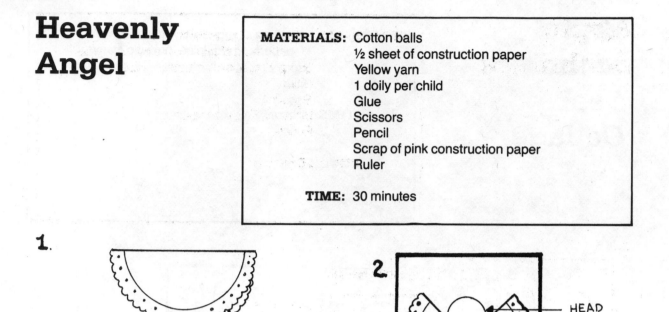

**MATERIALS:** Cotton balls
½ sheet of construction paper
Yellow yarn
1 doily per child
Glue
Scissors
Pencil
Scrap of pink construction paper
Ruler

**TIME:** 30 minutes

**1.**

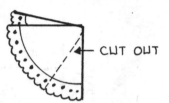

CUT OUT

Fold doily in half.

Fold doily in fourths.

**2.**

HEAD

WINGS

Glue doily wings on paper. Cut head from pink paper and glue onto paper. Draw triangle skirt with pencil and ruler.

**3.**

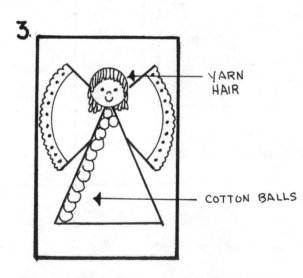

YARN HAIR

COTTON BALLS

Glue on yarn pieces for hair. Draw a face. Glue cotton balls on skirt.

**4.**

YARN HALO

Glue on piece of yarn for halo.

# Apple
# Bookmark

**MATERIALS:** 2'' × 2'' red construction paper
1'' × 6'' strip of green construction paper
Scrap of green construction paper
Glue
Scissors
Black and brown crayon
Pencil

**TIME:** 20 minutes

1.

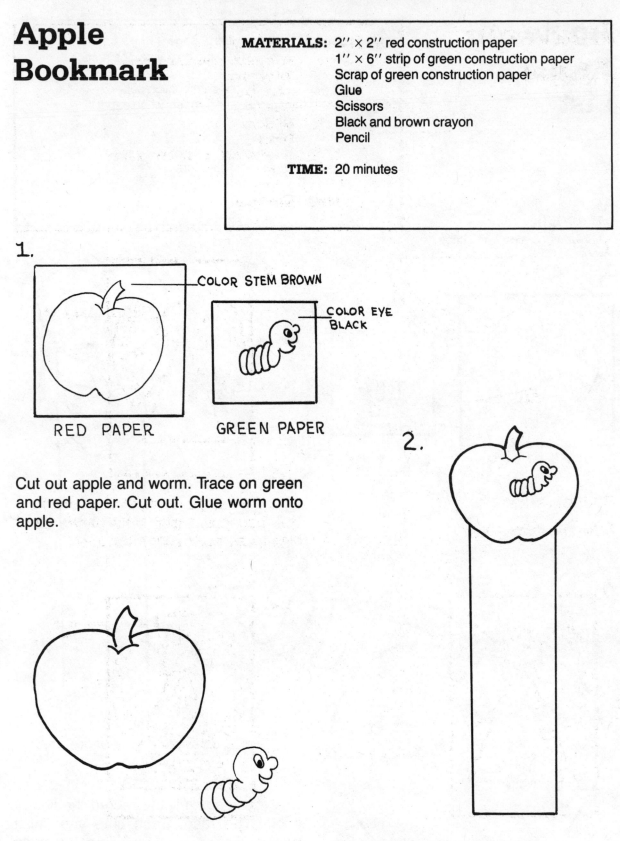

COLOR STEM BROWN

COLOR EYE
BLACK

RED PAPER

GREEN PAPER

Cut out apple and worm. Trace on green
and red paper. Cut out. Glue worm onto
apple.

2.

Glue apple on top of green strip.

From The Art Corner © 1979 Goodyear Publishing Company, Inc., Bonnie Flint Striebel, and
Ruth Beazell Forgan

# Apple
# Reading
# List

**MATERIALS:** *Apple pattern, page 113
1½″ × 12″ strip of green construction
   paper
3″ × 3″ red construction paper
Scrap of green construction paper
Glue
Scissors
Pencil
Brown and black crayon

**TIME:** 15 minutes

*TEACHER:
  This pattern is for book titles.

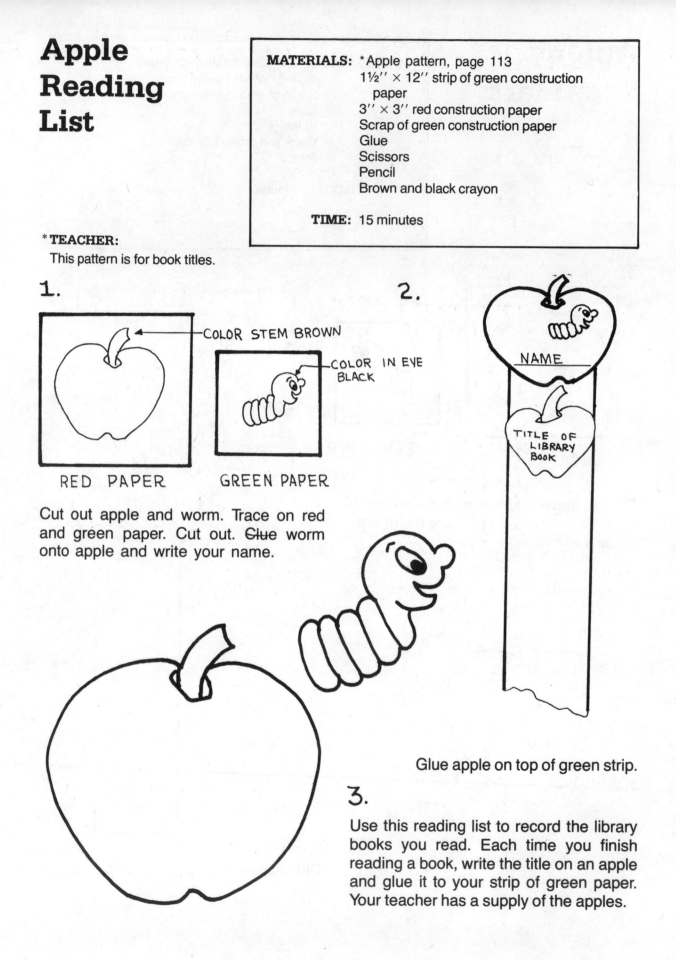

**1.**

COLOR STEM BROWN

COLOR IN EYE
BLACK

RED PAPER        GREEN PAPER

Cut out apple and worm. Trace on red
and green paper. Cut out. ~~Glue~~ worm
onto apple and write your name.

**2.**

NAME

TITLE OF
LIBRARY
BOOK

Glue apple on top of green strip.

**3.**

Use this reading list to record the library
books you read. Each time you finish
reading a book, write the title on an apple
and glue it to your strip of green paper.
Your teacher has a supply of the apples.

# Valentine People

**MATERIALS:** ½ sheet of construction paper for background
Scrap paper for hearts
Scissors
Glue
Pencil

**TIME:** 30 minutes

**1.**

Cut out hearts of different colors and sizes for all parts of a body. Plan your person.

**2.**

Glue on construction paper.

# Wheels

**MATERIALS:** 1 sheet of construction paper
Large scraps of paper
Scissors
Glue
Crayons

**TIME:** 30 minutes

**1.**

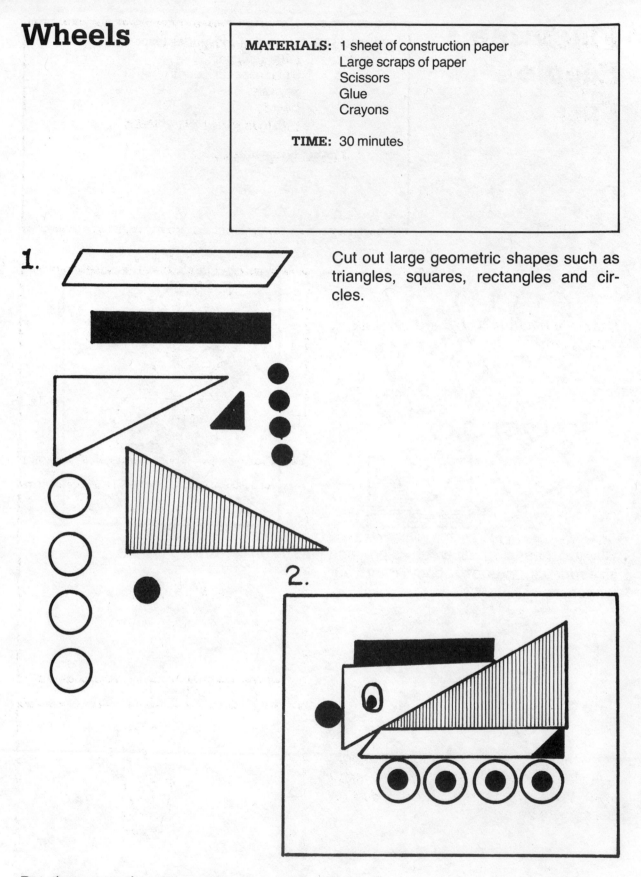

Cut out large geometric shapes such as triangles, squares, rectangles and circles.

**2.**

Put them together to create your own vehicle.

# Flash
# Card
# Fun

**MATERIALS:** Map pattern, page 114
Index cards
Glue
Scissors
Pencil
U.S. map with names of states

**TIME:** 1 hour or more

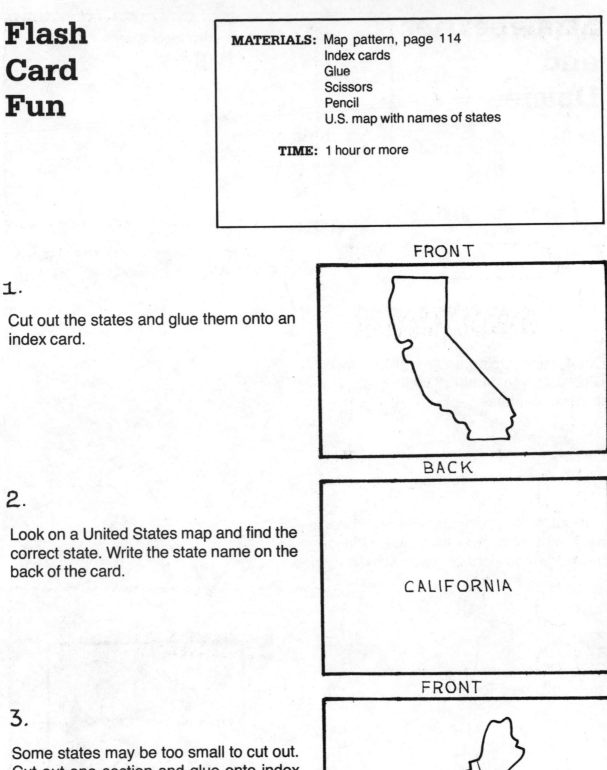

FRONT

BACK

CALIFORNIA

FRONT

**1.**

Cut out the states and glue them onto an index card.

**2.**

Look on a United States map and find the correct state. Write the state name on the back of the card.

**3.**

Some states may be too small to cut out. Cut out one section and glue onto index card. Write the names of the states on the back of the card.

*From The Art Corner © 1979 Goodyear Publishing Company, Inc., Bonnie Flint Striebel, and Ruth Beazell Forgan*

# Strawberries
# and
# Daisies

**MATERIALS:** ½ sheet yellow construction paper
½ sheet red construction paper
½ sheet of white construction paper
Scraps of yellow and green construction
    paper
Scissors
Pencil
Black crayon
Ruler

**TIME:** 1 hour

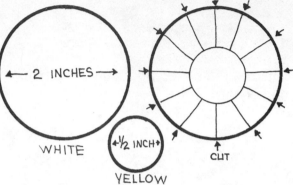

## 1.

Cut 4 white circles and 4 yellow circles. Glue yellow in center of white circle. Cut to yellow centers.

## 2.

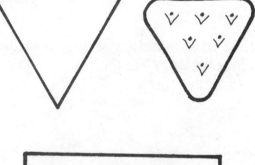

Cut out 4 red triangles. Round off corners with scissors. With black crayon make V's and dots on each strawberry.

## 3.

Glue shapes onto white paper. Add green triangles for leaves.

*From The Art Corner* © 1979 Goodyear Publishing Company, Inc., Bonnie Flint Striebel, and *Ruth Beazell Forgan*

# Construction Paper Snowflake

**MATERIALS:** *Construction paper
Scissors

**TIME:** 15 minutes

**\*TEACHER:**

Because of the heavy paper it is necessary
to cut the snowflake a bit differently than
when using thinner paper.
This project can be used for the Sparkle
Snowflake.

**1.**

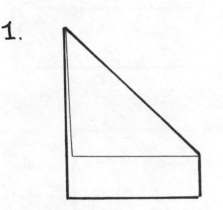

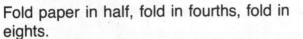

Fold paper in half, fold in fourths, fold in
eights.

**2.**

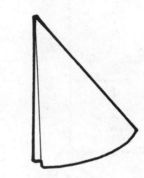

Trim off extra paper. Round edge.

**3.**

Open to fourths. Cut pieces from each
edge and center point.

**4.**

**5.**

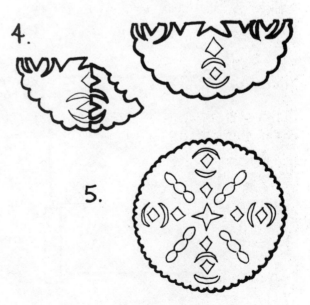

Fold one side toward center. Cut pieces
from edge. Repeat on other side.

*From* **The Art Corner** © 1979 *Goodyear Publishing Company, Inc., Bonnie Flint Striebel, and
Ruth Beazell Forgan*

# Easy Envelope

**MATERIALS:** 9" × 12" paper of any kind
Scissors
Glue

**TIME:** 15 minutes per envelope

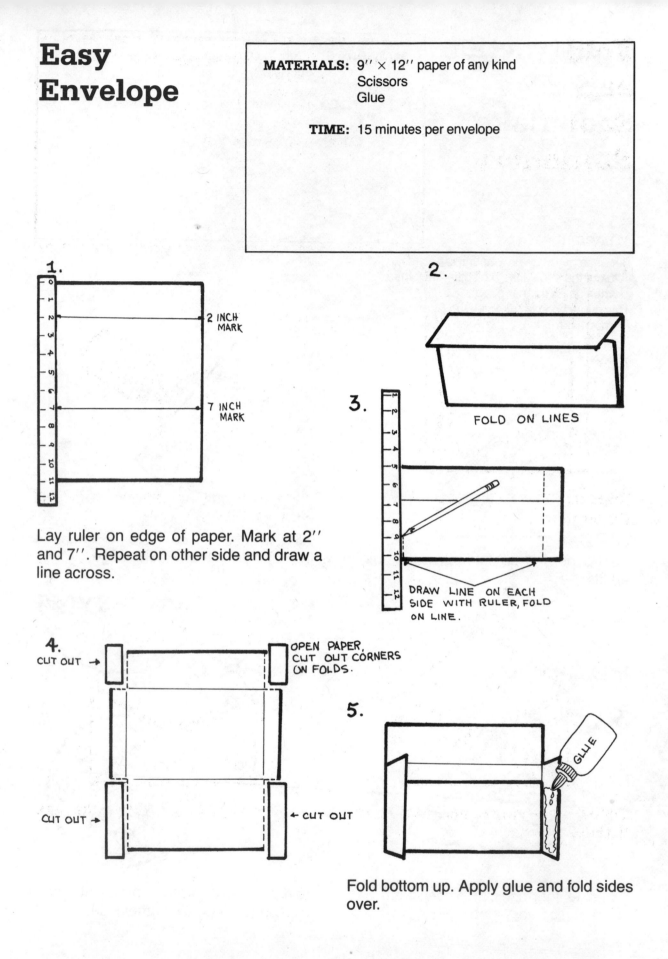

**1.**

2 INCH MARK

7 INCH MARK

Lay ruler on edge of paper. Mark at 2" and 7". Repeat on other side and draw a line across.

**2.**

FOLD ON LINES

**3.**

DRAW LINE ON EACH SIDE WITH RULER, FOLD ON LINE.

**4.**

CUT OUT →

OPEN PAPER, CUT OUT CORNERS ON FOLDS.

CUT OUT →

← CUT OUT

**5.**

GLUE

Fold bottom up. Apply glue and fold sides over.

# Fold
# and
# Seal
# Stationery

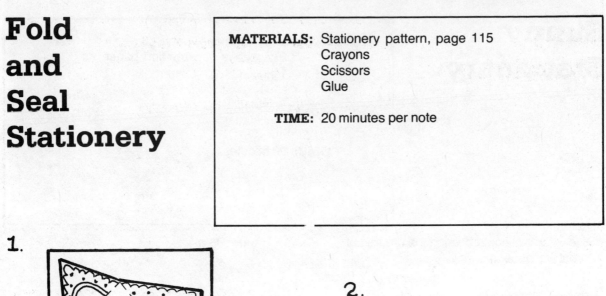

**MATERIALS:** Stationery pattern, page 115
Crayons
Scissors
Glue

**TIME:** 20 minutes per note

**1.**

Decorate flaps of envelope and circle.
Cut out the circle.

**2.**

Spread a thin layer of glue on the back of
the circle. Let dry.

**3.**

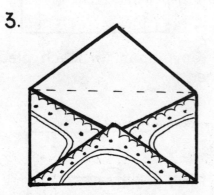

Cut out the envelope. Fold flaps on dot-
ted lines to center.

**4.**

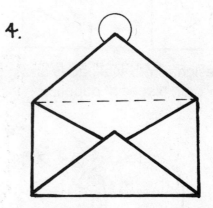

Lick *half* of circle and put on the large
flap.

# Sunny Stationery

**MATERIALS:** Easy envelope, page 68
2 pieces of construction paper
1 piece of typing paper
Glue
Scissors
*Wallpaper

**TIME:** 20 minutes

*Discarded wallpaper catalogues are free at
  most wallpaper stores.

1.
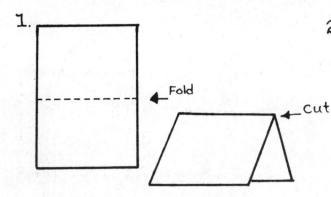

2.
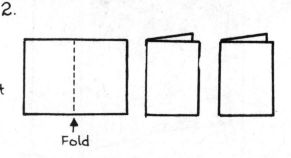

Fold both pieces of paper.

3.

Cut designs from wallpaper and glue to
front of both pieces of paper.

4.
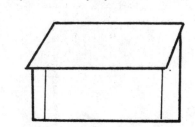

Make envelopes for each piece of
stationery.

5.

To make a sticker for your envelope, cut
out a circle, spread glue evenly and allow
to dry.

6.
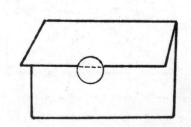

Lick half of the sticker and press on flap
of envelope.

# Quacker Greeting Card

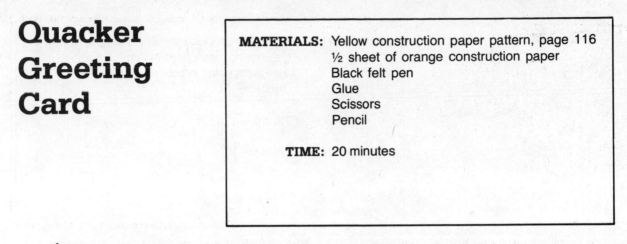

**MATERIALS:** Yellow construction paper pattern, page 116
½ sheet of orange construction paper
Black felt pen
Glue
Scissors
Pencil

**TIME:** 20 minutes

**1.**

Cut out duck. Cut out pattern for feet and duck bill.

**2.**

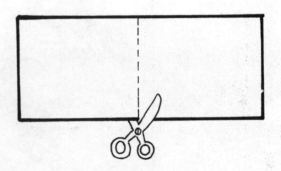

Fold orange paper in half and cut.

**3.**

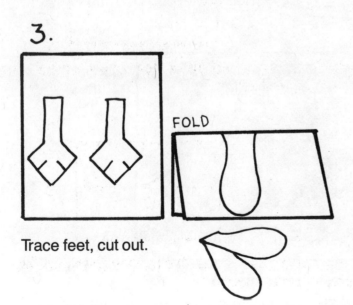

Trace feet, cut out.

Trace duck bill. *Make sure you do not cut fold.*

Glue on legs and duck bill. Open duck bill and write greetings.

*From* The Art Corner © *1979 Goodyear Publishing Company, Inc., Bonnie Flint Striebel, and Ruth Beazell Forgan*

# Paint
# and
# Newspaper
# Collage

**MATERIALS:** Large sheet of black construction paper
One sheet of newspaper
3 bright colors of tempera in squeeze
  bottles
Straw
Glue

**TIME:** 1 hour

1.

Put several spots of paint in one area.
Blow colors together with the straw. Fill
up the newspaper. Dry.

2.

Tear out the most interesting shapes and
glue onto the black paper.

# Want
# Ads
# Skyline

**MATERIALS:** 9″ × 12″ piece of white construction paper
1/4 sheet of want ads
1/4 sheet of newspaper
Black and yellow tempera paint
Glue
Scissors
2 jar lids for paint
Paint brush

**TIME:** 1 hour

## 1.

Wad newspaper section into a ball. Dip into black paint and texture white paper.

## 2.

Cut out skyline and glue to textured paper.

## 3.

Outline buildings in black. Add yellow for windows and moon.

*From* The Art Corner © *1979 Goodyear Publishing Company, Inc., Bonnie Flint Striebel, and Ruth Beazell Forgan*

# School Play Costumes

**MATERIALS:** Newspapers
Glue
Paper clips
Stapler
Felt pens or crayons
Grocery sacks in assorted sizes
Construction paper scraps if desired

**TIME:** 30 minutes daily for several days

**1.**

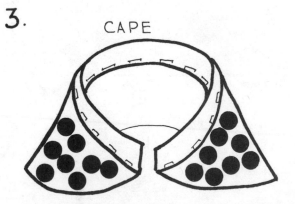

SKIRT

Fold a large sheet of newspaper into a long strip. Staple at each end. Pleat several newspapers and staple to the strip. Decorate. Paper clip to keep on.

**2.**

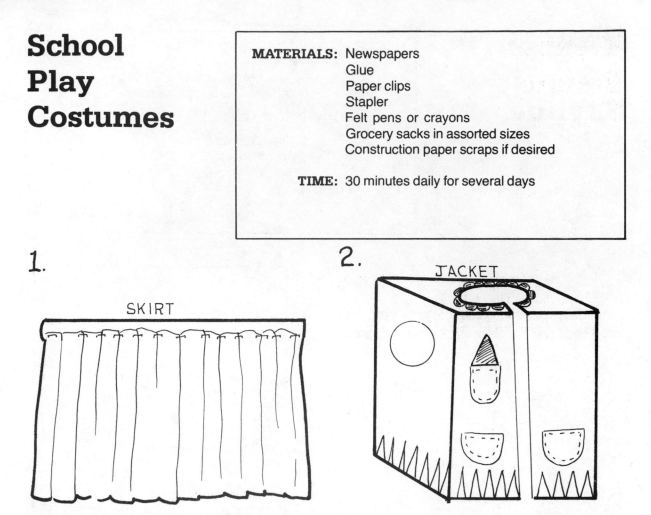

JACKET

Use a large grocery sack. Cut neckhole, armholes, and fringe. Decorate with scraps of construction paper, felt pens or crayons.

**3.**

CAPE

Fold newspaper into a long strip. Staple another sheet to strip. Trim corners. Decorate. Paper clip to keep on.

**4.**

HAT

Use smaller sacks to make hats. Decorate.

*From The Art Corner © 1979 Goodyear Publishing Company, Inc., Bonnie Flint Striebel, and Ruth Beazell Forgan*

# Kleenex
# Bouquet

MATERIALS: 3 facial tissues
Scissors
Pipe cleaner

TIME: 30 minutes

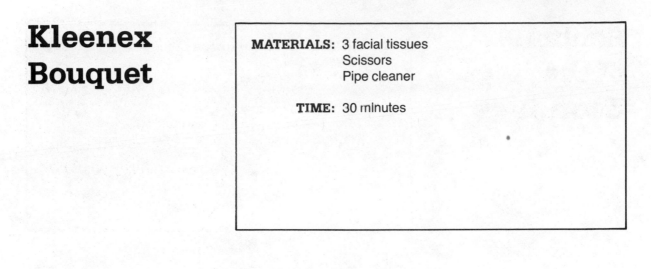

**1.**

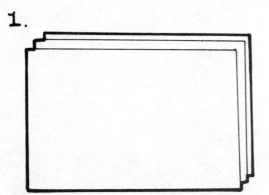

Open tissues and lay flat.

**2.**

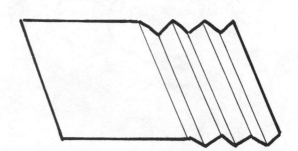

Accordion fold tissues.

**3.**

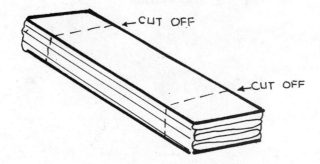

← CUT OFF

← CUT OFF

**4.**

Tie tightly in the center with pipe cleaner. Spread tissue open. Pull each layer carefully towards the center.

**From The Art Corner** © 1979 Goodyear Publishing Company, Inc., Bonnie Flint Striebel, and Ruth Beazell Forgan

# Animals
## of the
## Zoo

**MATERIALS:** White construction paper pattern page 117
Scissors
Crayons or felt pens

**TIME:** 30 minutes

**1.**

Color patterns. Cut out.

**2.**

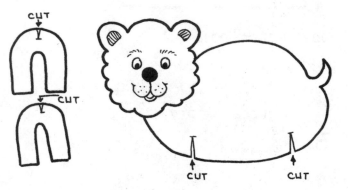

Cut slits in legs and body.

**3.**

Put legs on animals.

# Frame
# Me

**MATERIALS:** Discarded wallpaper book
Luncheon size paper plate
Scissors
Glue
Photograph of self

**TIME:** 30 minutes

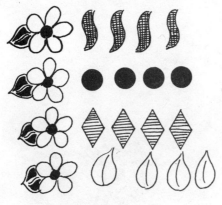

## 1.

Select designs from old wallpaper. Cut out.

## 2.

Glue designs onto paper plate in a pretty arrangement.

## 3.

Glue photograph in the center.

*From The Art Corner* © *1979 Goodyear Publishing Company, Inc., Bonnie Flint Striebel, and Ruth Beazell Forgan*

# Ditto
# Me

**MATERIALS:** Drawing paper
Scissors
Glue
Fabric or scraps of gift wrap
Yellow or brown yarn

**TIME:** 30–45 minutes

**1.**

Draw a picture of yourself without hair.

**2.**

Cut out clothes to dress yourself.

**3.**

Put glue on the top of the head and lay on yarn.

**4.**

Put glue on the paper and lay on the clothing.

# Fancy
# Paint
# Shirt

**MATERIALS:**  Dad's shirt
Fabric pieces
Glue
Scissors
Felt pens
Newspapers for cover

**TIME:**  Spare time

**1.**

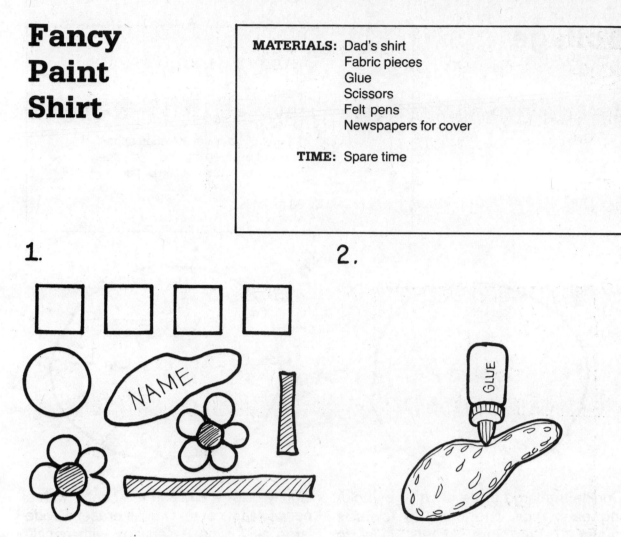

Cut shapes and patterns out of material.

**2.**

Spread glue on back of shape or pattern.

**3.**

Glue shapes on shirt.

**4.**

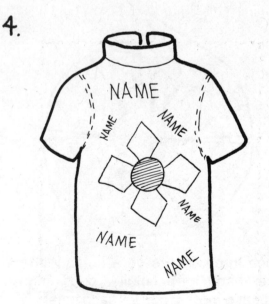

Decorate with felt pens.

# Foilage

**MATERIALS:** Tinfoil
      1 piece 12″ × 12″
      1 piece 9″ × 12″
Pencil
Glue
Scissors
1 sheet of black construction paper
½ sheet of green construction paper
Scrap of red construction paper

**TIME:** 30 minutes

**1.**

Crinkle the large piece of tinfoil by holding each side and pushing towards center. Flatten. Turn corners under to form circle.

**2.**

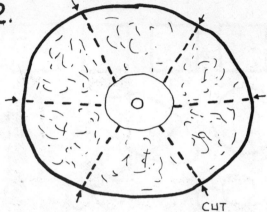

Lightly draw a circle in the center with a pencil. Mark center with an eraser. Divide large circle into 6 sections with pencil. Cut to small circle.

**3.**

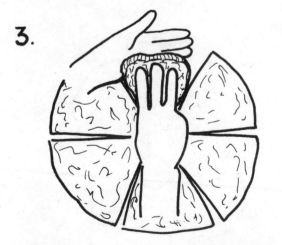

Place three fingers on a petal. With the other hand form tinfoil around fingers. Repeat 5 more times for each petal.

**4.**

Make another flower exactly the same from a smaller piece of foil. Glue both together. Glue on black paper. Cut stem and leaves. Make a red center with smaller green circle on top.

# Chain
# of
# Foil

**MATERIALS:** 6″ × 6″ pieces of tinfoil

**TIME:** 30 minutes depending upon the length of chain

**1.**

Fold tinfoil in half. Fold in half again. Fold in half once again.

**2.**

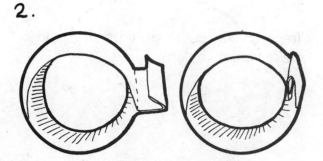

Make a circle. Match the ends together. Make small fold, pinch. Make another small fold and pinch again.

**3.**

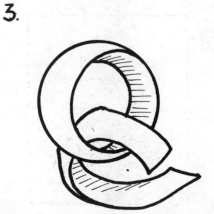

Fold another piece of foil. Put through the first circle, before you pinch.

**4.**

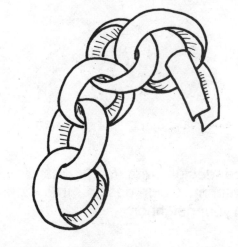

Make chain as long as you want. Happy chain making!

# Stenciled Gift Wrap

**MATERIALS:** * Plastic butter dish lid or coffee can lid
Scissors
Felt pens
Cookie cutter if desired
Newsprint
Pen

**TIME:** 20 minutes

**\* TEACHER:**
Save stencils for other projects

## 1.

Trace cookie cutter on lid with a pen or make your own design.

## 2.

Cut through side of lid with scissors. Cut out design carefully.

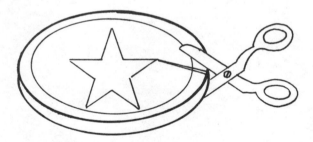

## 3.

Trace design with magic marker onto newsprint. Color design. Trade stencils with your neighbor.

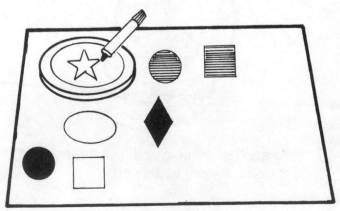

# Birthday Crown

**MATERIALS:** Five 1½'' strips of construction paper
Large scrap of construction paper
Glue/Stapler
Scissors
Crayons
Stencils if desired

**TIME:** 40 minutes

**1.**

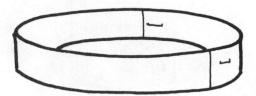

Staple strip to fit head.

**2.**

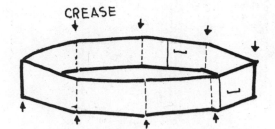

Crease in half, fourths and eighths.

**3.**

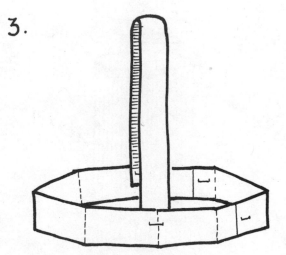

Staple strips to creases.

**4.**

Cut out design or use stencil to write Happy Birthday. Staple to hat.

From The Art Corner © 1979 Goodyear Publishing Company, Inc., *Bonnie Flint Striebel, and Ruth Beazell Forgan*

# The Toothpick's Toothpick

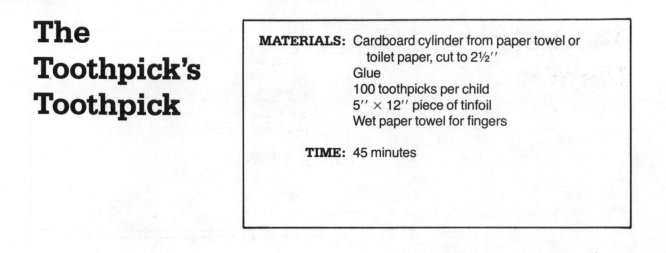

**MATERIALS:** Cardboard cylinder from paper towel or toilet paper, cut to 2½"
Glue
100 toothpicks per child
5" × 12" piece of tinfoil
Wet paper towel for fingers

**TIME:** 45 minutes

**1.**

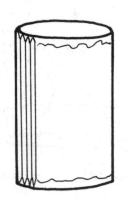

Cover cardboard cylinder with glue. Lay toothpicks up and down (vertically) around cylinder.

**2.**

Cover edge of opening with glue. Lay toothpicks side by side across the opening to cover.

**3.**

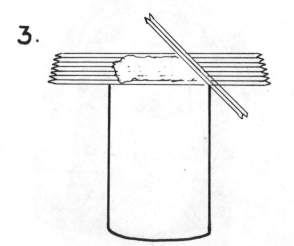

Drizzle glue across the center of the first layer of toothpicks. Lay toothpicks across in the opposite direction. Let dry.

**4.**

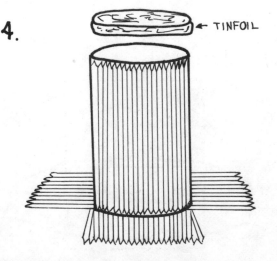

← TINFOIL

Form a piece of tinfoil to the size of the opening. Place in the bottom of container so toothpicks will stand tall.

# Toothpick Planter

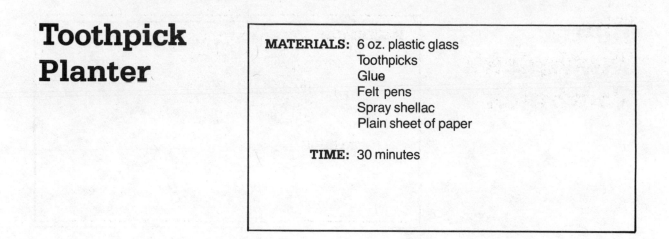

**MATERIALS:** 6 oz. plastic glass
Toothpicks
Glue
Felt pens
Spray shellac
Plain sheet of paper

**TIME:** 30 minutes

1.

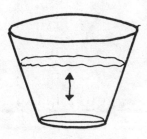

Cover ¾ glass with glue.

2.

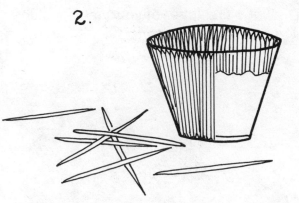

Lay toothpicks side by side to cover the whole glass. Let dry for a few minutes.

3.

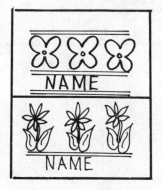

Use your plain sheet of paper and draw the design you want to put on your glass.

4.

Draw your design on the glass. Write your name around the bottom and spray shellac.

*From* The Art Corner © *1979 Goodyear Publishing Company, Inc., Bonnie Flint Striebel, and Ruth Beazell Forgan*

# Letter Puppets

**MATERIALS:** ½ sheet of heavy paper
Crayons or felt pens
Pencil
Stapler
Straws
Ruler

**TIME:** 30 minutes

**1.**

Draw the first letter of your name making it as large as the paper.

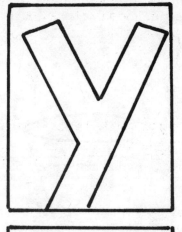

**2.**

Using your crayons or felt pens, make the letter look like a person or animal.

**3.**

Cut letter out and staple a straw to the letter to make a puppet.

# Cool
# Collage

**MATERIALS:** Straws—precut by the teacher into various lengths
Jar lid for glue
Wet paper towel
Glue    Ruler
Scissors  Pencil

1 sheet of construction paper
½ sheet of construction paper in contrasting color

**TIME:** 45 minutes

**TEACHER:**

For intermediate grades, geometric shapes can be used and the entire shape or shapes may be filled in.

## 1.

Draw 3 numerals between 1 and 9 in any direction, and any size. Leave space between.

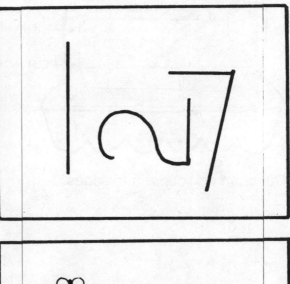

## 2.

Dip end of cut straws in glue. Stand on end on each side of the line. Straws will be different lengths.

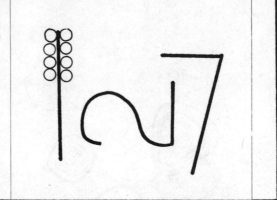

## 3.

Repeat for each numeral. Let dry.

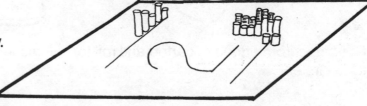

*From The Art Corner* © 1979 Goodyear Publishing Company, Inc., Bonnie Flint Striebel, and *Ruth Beazell Forgan*

# Egg
# Carton
# Sculpture

**MATERIALS:** Egg carton
Toothpicks
Scissors

**TIME:** 1 hour or more if desired

**1.**

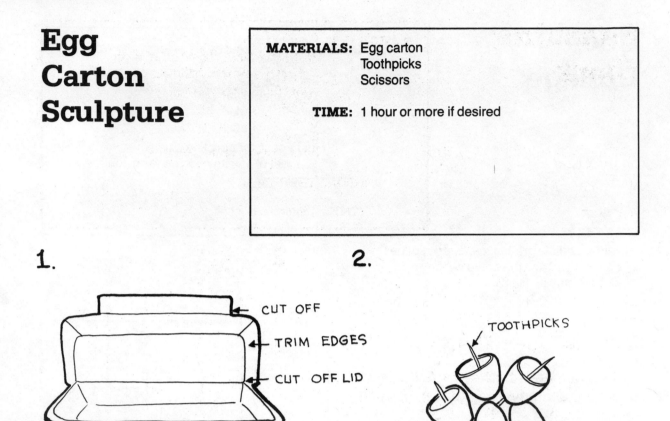

CUT OFF

TRIM EDGES

CUT OFF LID

Cut apart egg cups. Trim edges.

**2.**

TOOTHPICKS

Make base from the lid of egg carton.
Use toothpicks to hold egg cups together.

**3.**

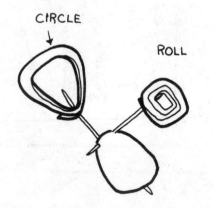

CIRCLE

ROLL

Cut strips from edges of carton and roll to
form circles.

**4.**

Finished sculpture.

*From* The Art Corner © *1979 Goodyear Publishing Company, Inc., Bonnie Flint Striebel, and
Ruth Beazell Forgan*

# Sunshine Clock

**MATERIALS:** 1 paper plate
¼ sheet of black construction paper
1 sheet of yellow construction paper with
   sunshine pattern, page 118
1 brad
Glue
Scissors
Black crayon or felt pens

**TIME:** 30 minutes

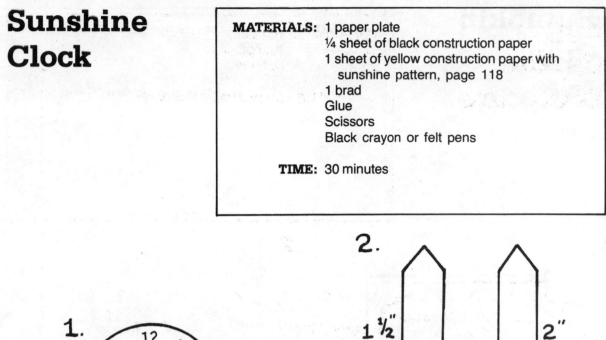

**1.**

Draw numbers on the front of the plate.
Draw eyes, nose, and a happy mouth.

**2.**

1½″     2″

Cut out a 1½″ and a 2″ strip of black for
hands of the clock.

**3.**

Fasten clock hands to plate with the brad.
It should be attached on the nose.

**4.**

Cut out yellow triangles and glue around
the outside of the plate.

# Pumpkin Cup

**MATERIALS:** 4 orange construction paper circles, pattern page 119
Glue
Scissors
1″ × 9″ strip of green construction paper

**TIME:** 30 minutes

**1.**

Draw faces on pumpkins and cut out.

**2.**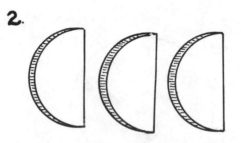

Fold each circle in half with face inside.

**3.**

Glue, lay folded circle on top. Do the same thing for the other 2 circles.

**4.**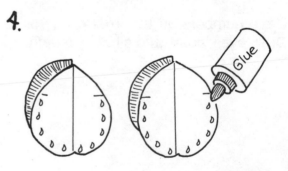

Glue on edges and press together.

Glue on handle.

# Egg
# Cup
# Flower

**MATERIALS:** 2 egg carton cups
Scissors
Glue
½ sheet of construction paper
½ sheet of green construction paper for
stems and leaves

**TIME:** 30 minutes

1.

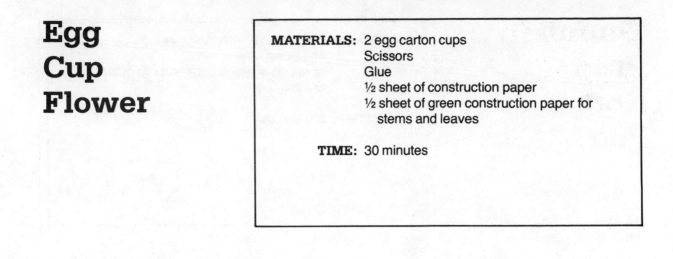

Cup 1.

Cup 2.

Cut

Cut at each
arrow.

3.

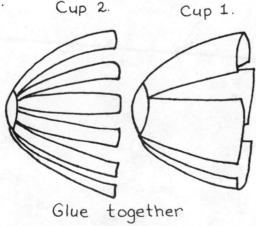

Cup 2.    Cup 1.

Glue  together

4.

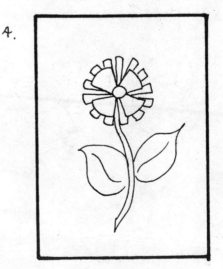

From The Art Corner © 1979 Goodyear Publishing Company, Inc., Bonnie Flint Striebel, and
Ruth Beazell Forgan

# Thumb Print Note Pad

**MATERIALS:** * Stamp pad—colors or black
Felt pens
Note pad or typing paper cut into quarters
Scratch paper

**TIME:** 30 minutes

**TEACHER:**

Make paint pad by mixing soap, tempera, and water. Do not make it too thin. Fold paper towel into quarters. Put about ½ teaspoon of tempera on pad and spread it around. The paint is more effective if it is on the dry side. Thumb prints should be light.

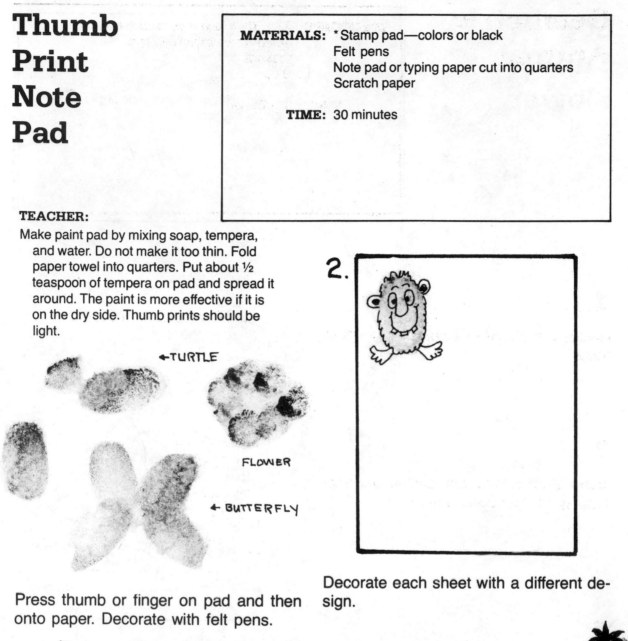

←TURTLE

FLOWER

← BUTTERFLY

2.

Press thumb or finger on pad and then onto paper. Decorate with felt pens.

Decorate each sheet with a different design.

3.

Here are some ideas for you.

# Geometric Animal

**MATERIALS:** 9″ × 12″ piece of construction paper
Scraps of construction paper
Crayons
Glue

**TIME:** 30 minutes

## 1.

Decide what kind of animal you want to make.

EXAMPLE: HORSE

## 2.

Tear triangles, squares, circles, and rectangles from scraps of paper.

## 3.

Paste on paper to form animal. Make eyes, nose, mouth, and any other decorations you want.

From The Art Corner © 1979 Goodyear Publishing Company, Inc., Bonnie Flint Striebel, and Ruth Beazell Forgan

# Daffy Dog

**MATERIALS:** Daffy Dog pattern, page 120
Crayons
Scissors
Ruler
Pencil

**TIME:** 30 minutes

1.

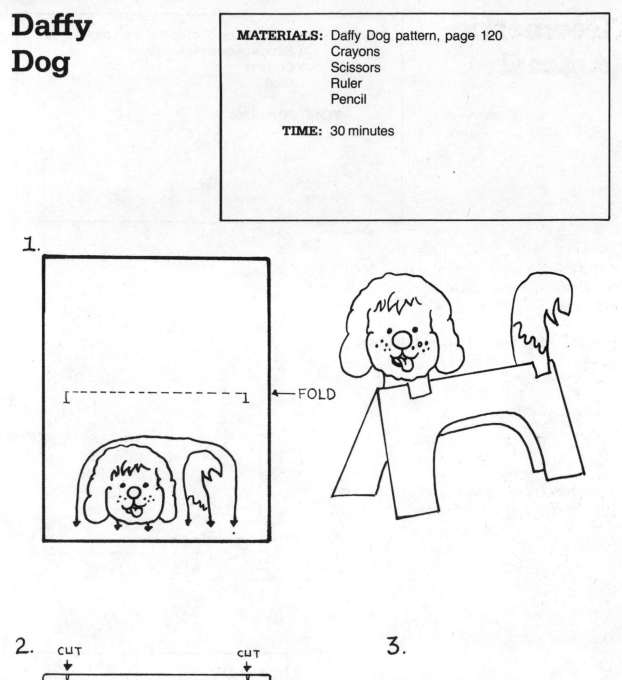

← FOLD

2.

CUT    CUT

← CUT OFF 1 INCH →

3.

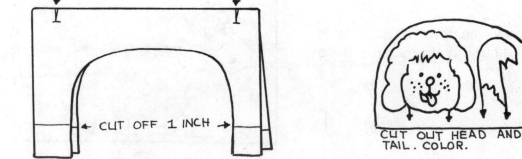

CUT OUT HEAD AND TAIL. COLOR.

# Geometric Cartoons

**MATERIALS:** Pencil
White drawing paper
Crayons

**TIME:** 30 minutes

Use your pencil to draw the geometric shapes to make an animal. Then outline the shapes, make eyes, mouths, and tails. Color with your crayons.

1.

2.

3.

4.

# Ring
# of
# Health

**MATERIALS:** Fruits and vegetables pattern, pages 121-23
9″ × 12″ piece of green construction paper
Crayons
Scissors
Glue

**TIME:** 45 minutes

**1.**

Color the fruits and vegetables. Cut them out.

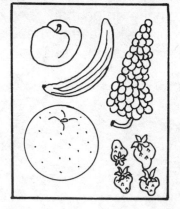

**2.**

Cut corners from green paper. Draw a circle in the middle of the paper and cut it out.

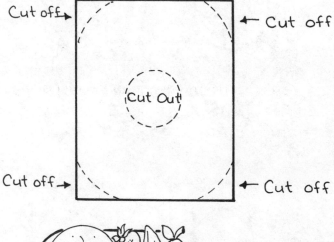

**3.**

Glue the fruits and vegetables around the ring to make your Ring of Health.

*From* The Art Corner © *1979 Goodyear Publishing Company, Inc., Bonnie Flint Striebel, and Ruth Beazell Forgan*

# Lantern

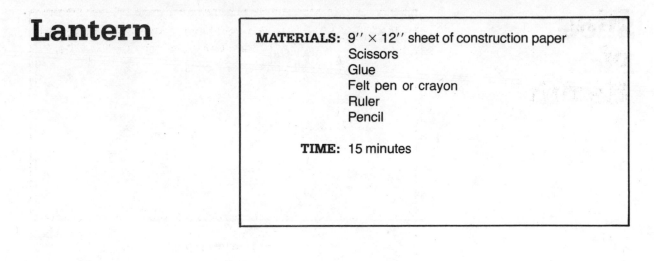

MATERIALS: 9″ × 12″ sheet of construction paper
Scissors
Glue
Felt pen or crayon
Ruler
Pencil

TIME: 15 minutes

**1.**

← CUT OFF

Cut 1″ strip from paper for the handle. Use crayons and decorate the rest of the page.

**2.**

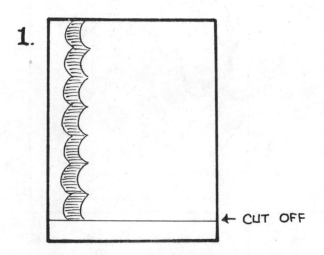

Fold paper in half with design on the outside.

**3.**

CUT

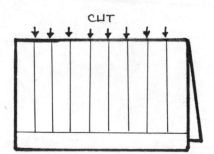

Measure 1″ across bottom and draw line. Measure and draw 1″ lines across the page. Cut to the line.

**4.**

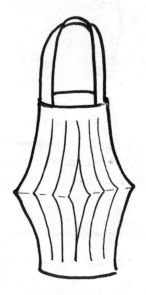

Open and glue edges together. Glue on handle.

# Shoe
# Fish

**MATERIALS:** Paper
Scissors
Felt pens or crayons

**TIME:** 30 minutes

**2.**

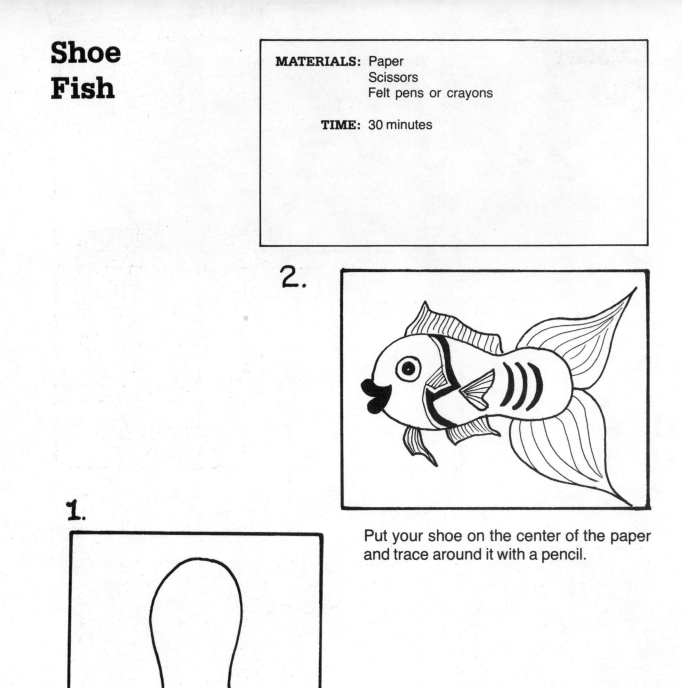

Put your shoe on the center of the paper and trace around it with a pencil.

**1.**

Use crayons or felt pens to decorate.

# Figure Fun

**MATERIALS:** Three ½ sheets of 9″ × 6″ white
construction paper
Stapler
Crayons and felt pens
Scissors
Ruler
Pencil

**TIME:** 45 minutes

1.

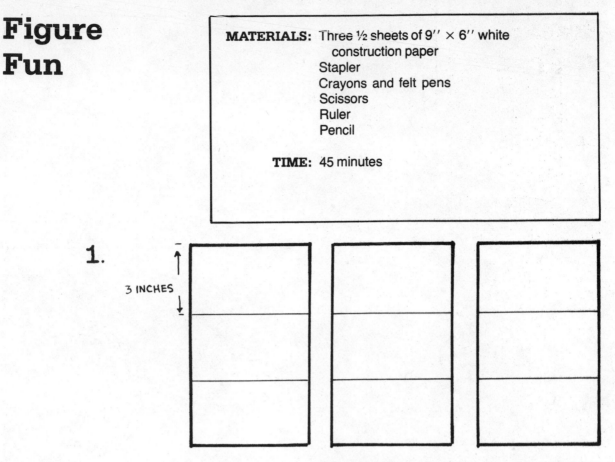

3 INCHES

Divide each sheet of paper into three 3″ sections with ruler.

2.

Draw three silly characters, one on each page. Draw a head in the top section. Draw a body and arms in the middle section. Draw legs and feet in the bottom section.

3.

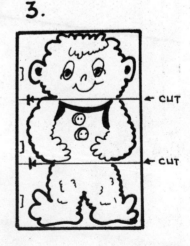

CUT

CUT

Staple sheets together. Cut each page on lines almost to the edge. Mix and match your figures.

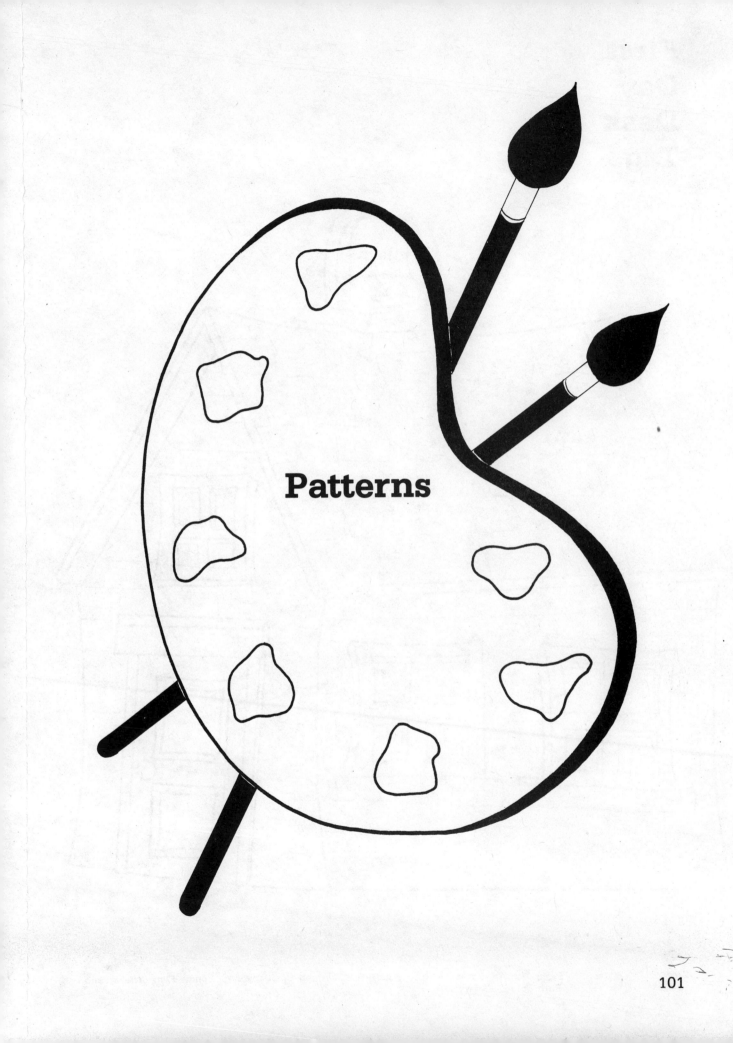

# Patterns

# First
# Day
## Desk
## Tags

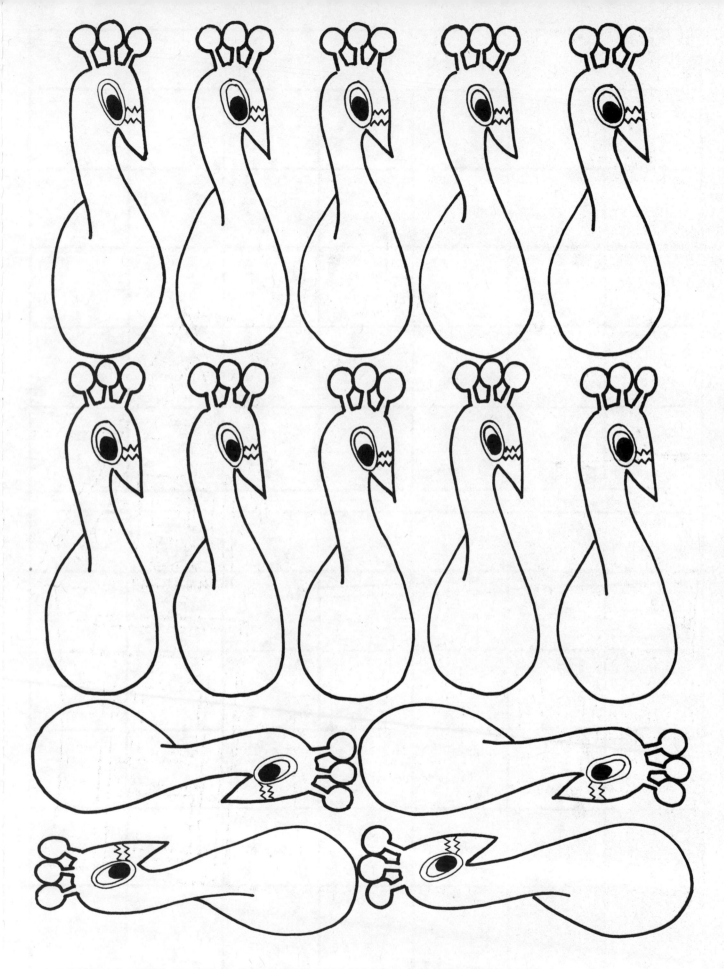

CALENDAR

| | | | | | | |
|---|---|---|---|---|---|---|
| | | | | | | |
| | | | | | | |
| | | | | | | |
| | | | | | | |

CALENDAR

| | | | | | | |
|---|---|---|---|---|---|---|
| | | | | | | |
| | | | | | | |
| | | | | | | |
| | | | | | | |

# Little
# Benny

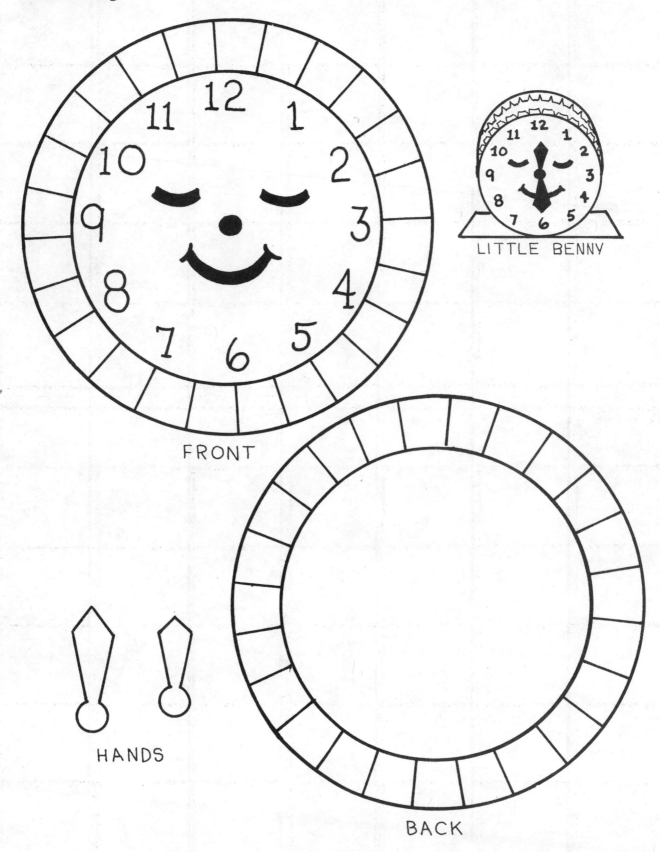

FRONT

LITTLE BENNY

HANDS

BACK

106

# Lincoln
# Silhouette

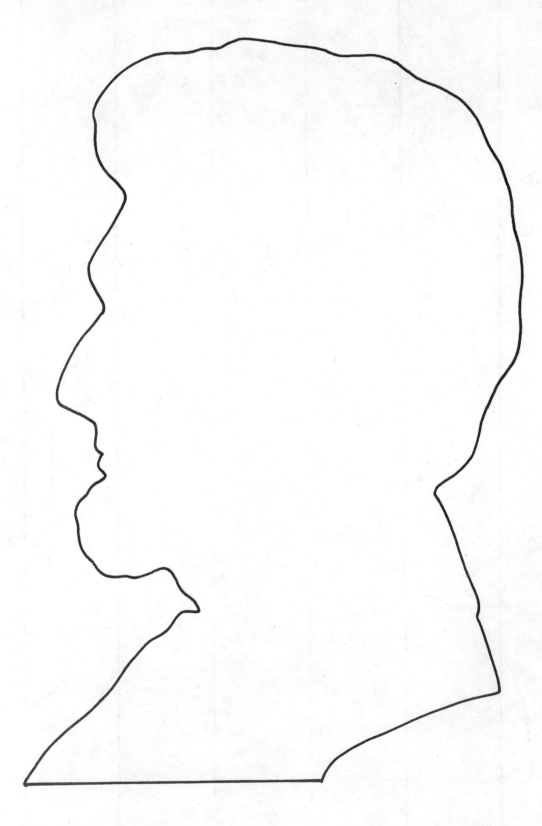

# Washington
# Silhouette

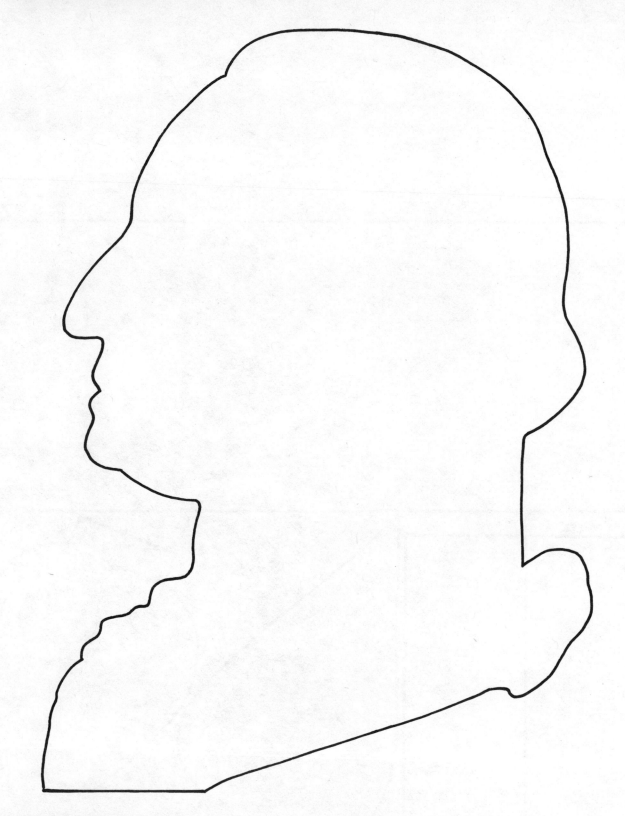

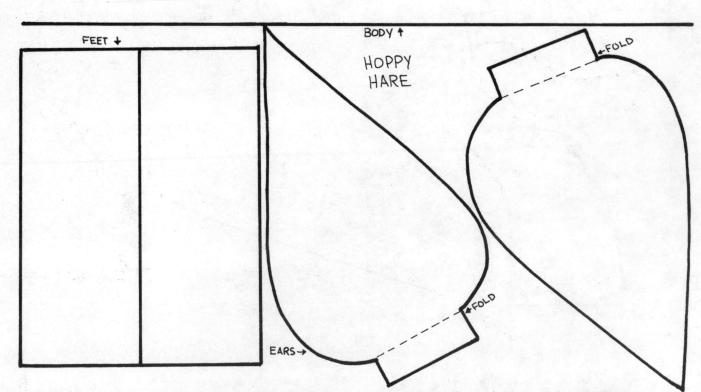

FEET ↓

BODY ↑

HOPPY HARE

←FOLD

←FOLD

EARS→

# Cupid
# Mobile

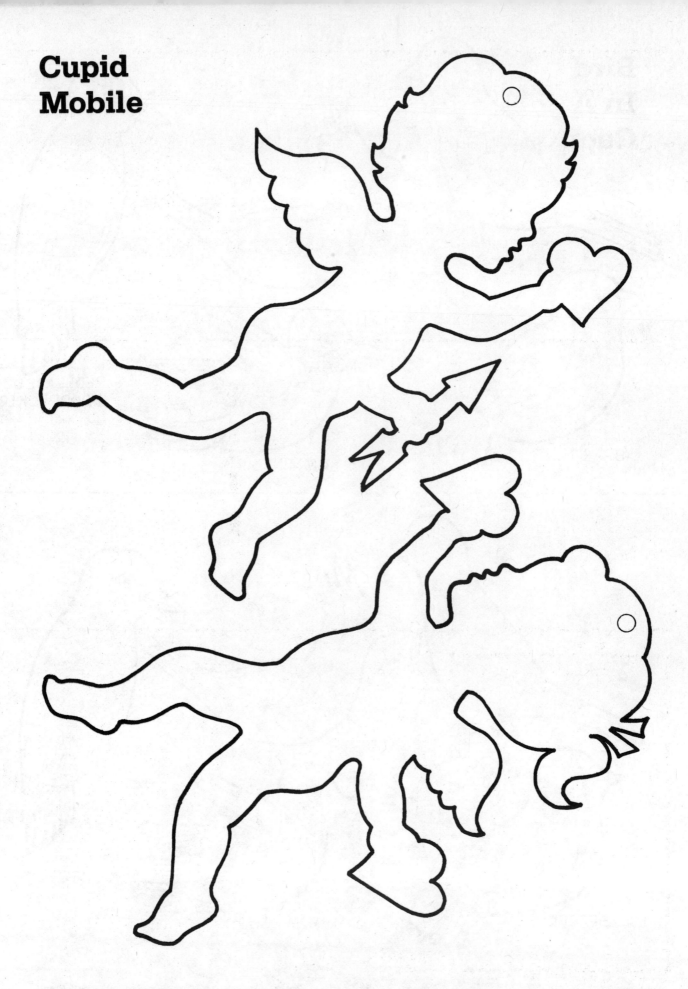

# Bird
# In A
# Cage

ROBIN

CARDINAL

SPARROW

HUMMINGBIRD

REDHEADED
WOODPECKER

ROBIN

CARDINAL

SPARROW

HUMMINGBIRD

REDHEADED
WOODPECKER

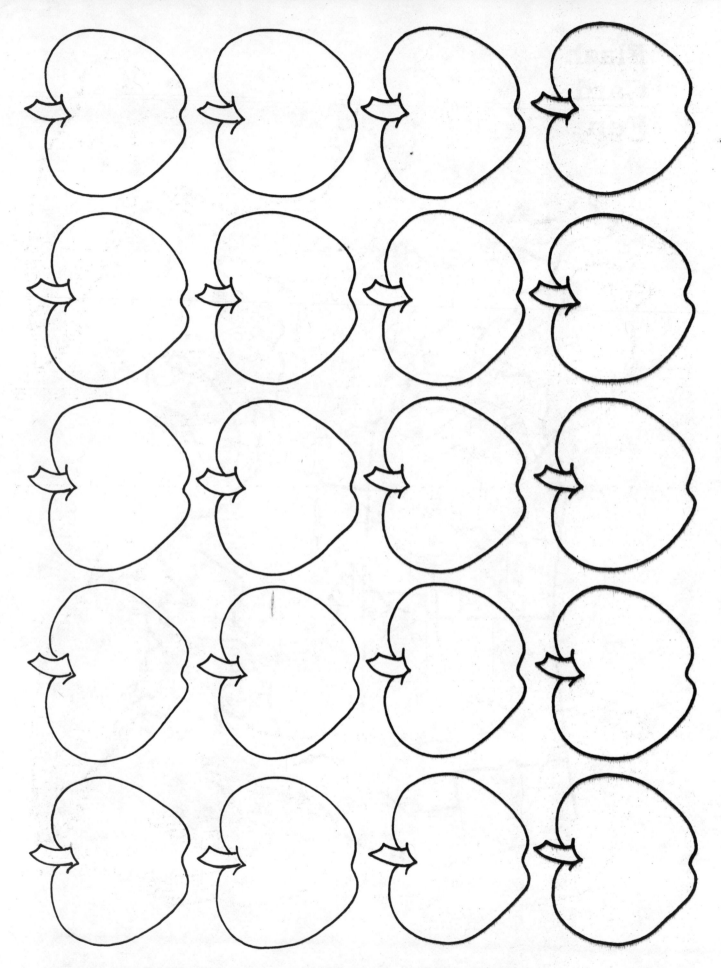

# Flash
# Card
# Fun

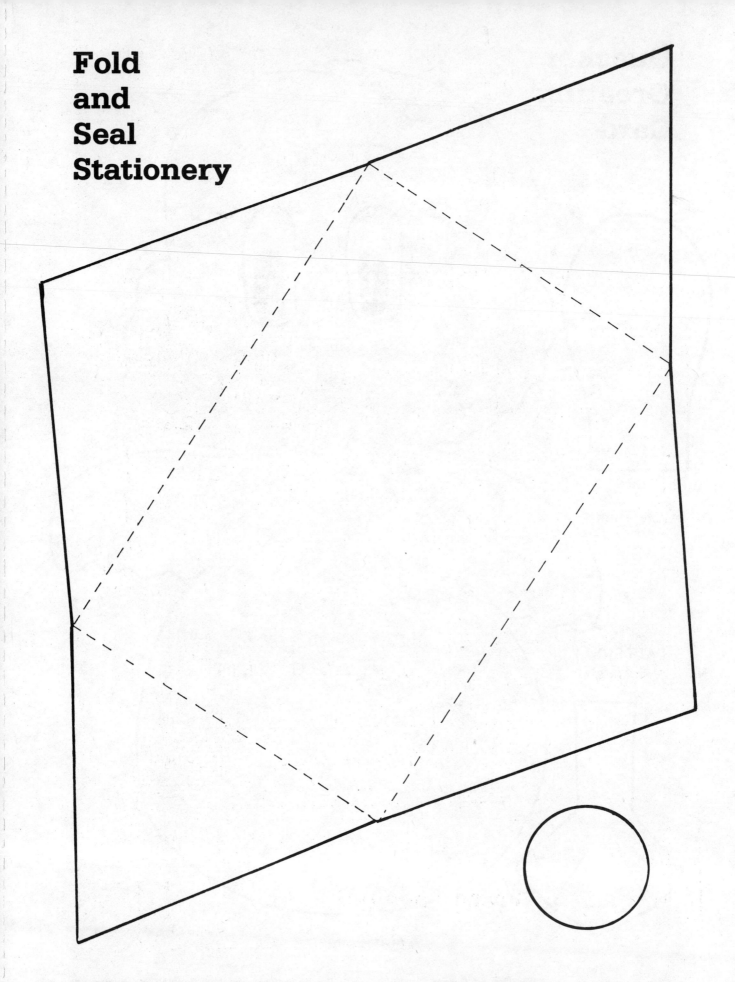

# Fold
# and
# Seal
# Stationery

# Quacker Greeting Card

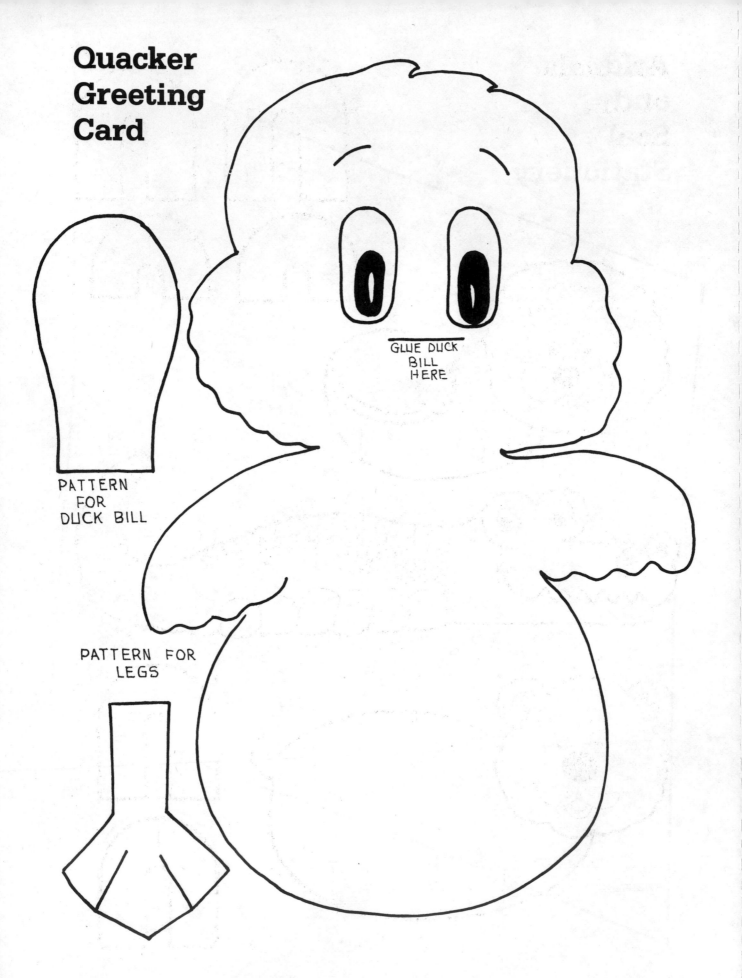

PATTERN
FOR
DUCK BILL

GLUE DUCK
BILL
HERE

PATTERN FOR
LEGS

# Animals
## of the
## Zoo

From The Art Corner © 1979 Goodyear Publishing Company, Inc., Bonnie Flint Striebel, and Ruth Beazell Forgan

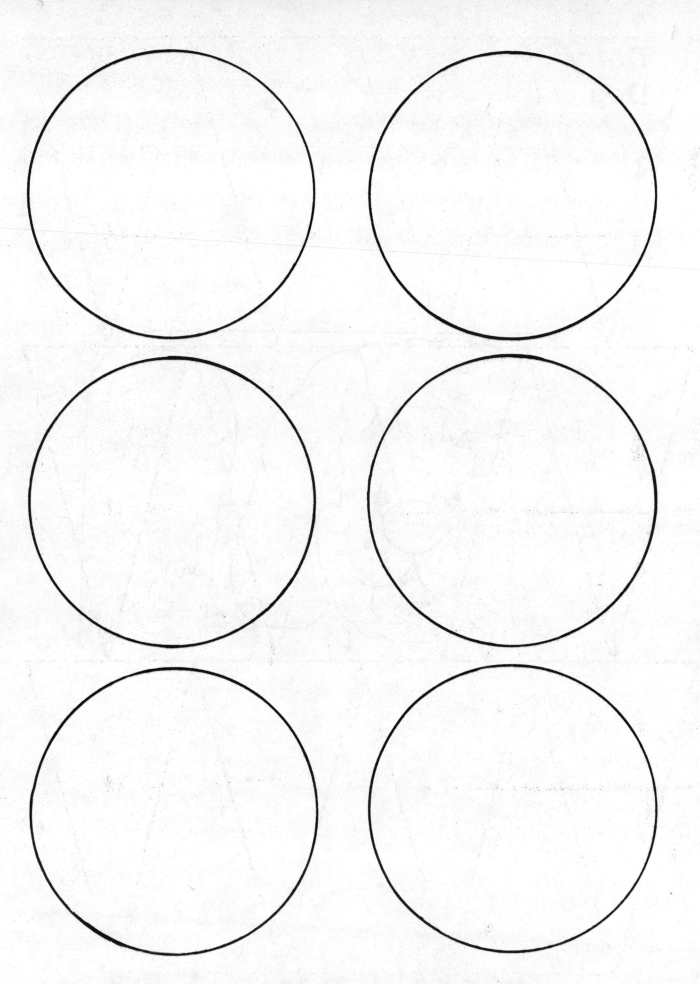

119

# Daffy
# Dog

From The Art Corner © 1979 Goodyear Publishing Company, Inc., Bonnie Flint Striebel, and Ruth Beazell Forgan

# Ring of Health

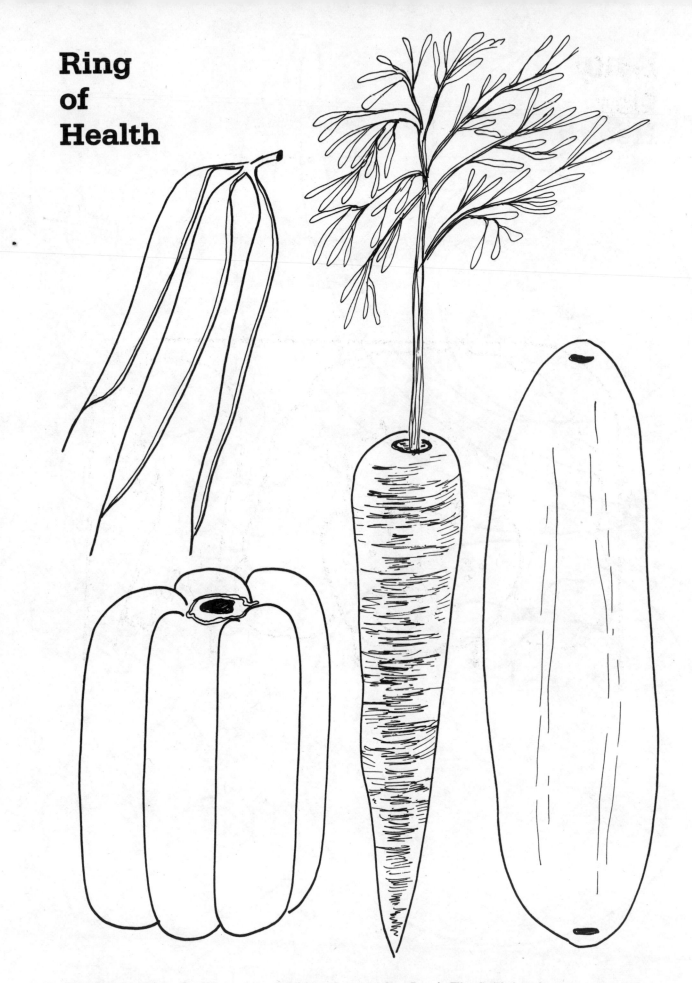

From The Art Corner © 1979 Goodyear Publishing Company, Inc., Bonnie Flint Striebel, and
*Ruth Beazell Forgan*

# Ring
# of
# Health

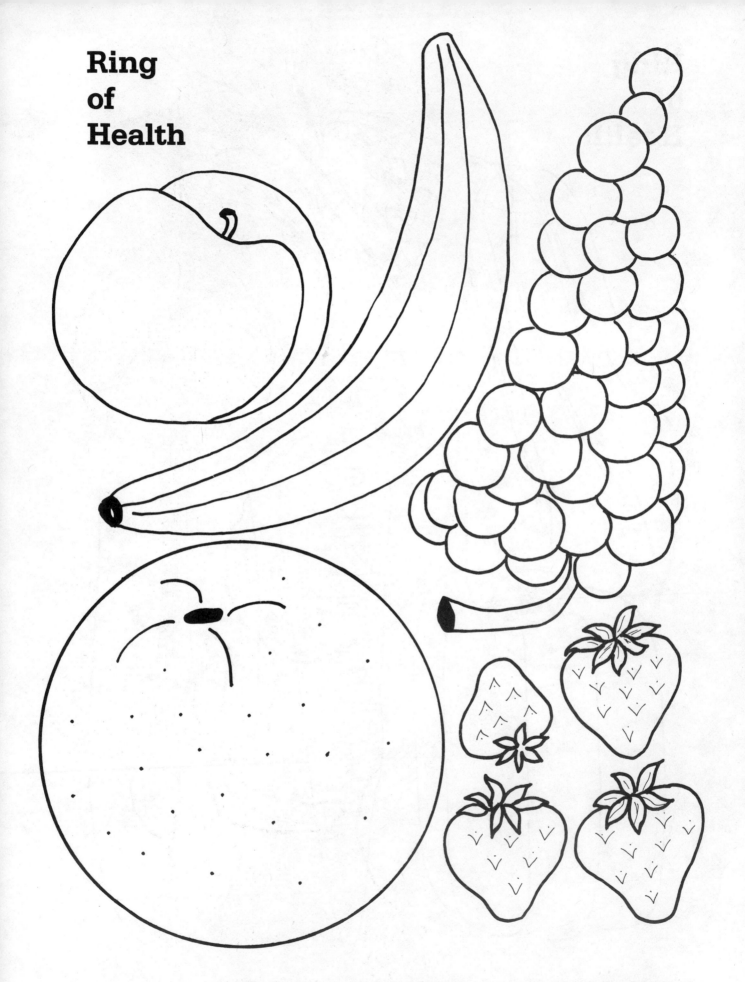

# Ring of Health

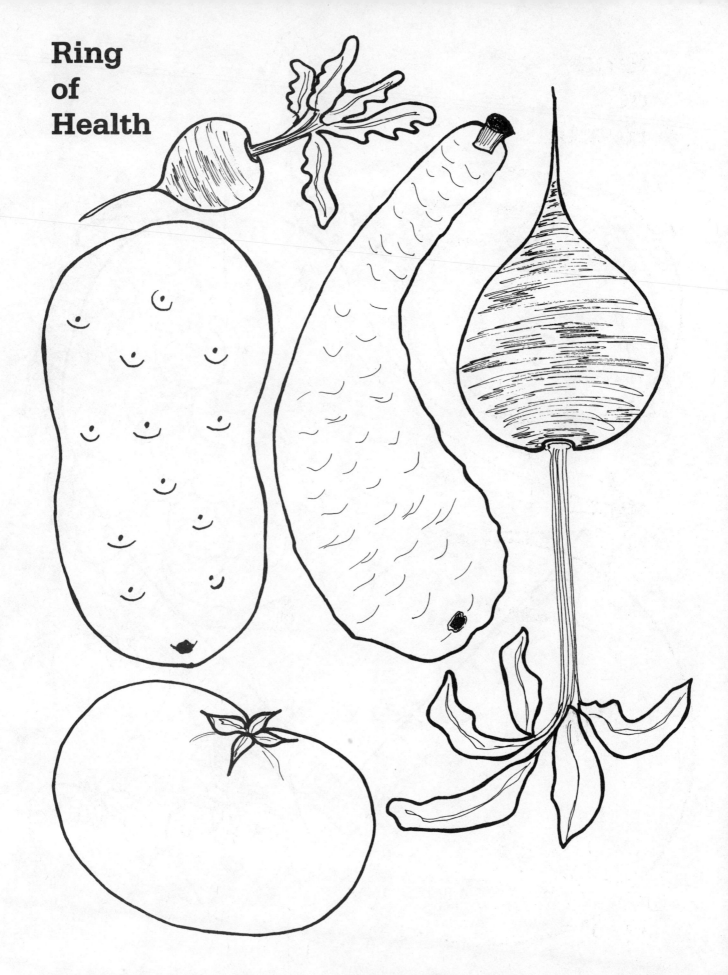

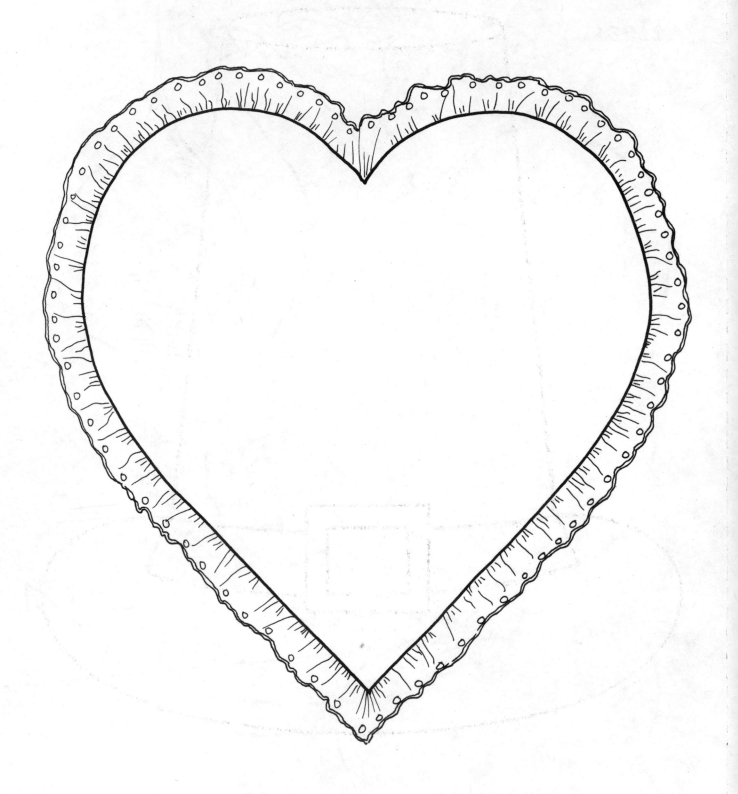

From The Art Corner © 1979 Goodyear Publishing Company, Inc., Bonnie Flint Striebel, and Ruth Beazell Forgan

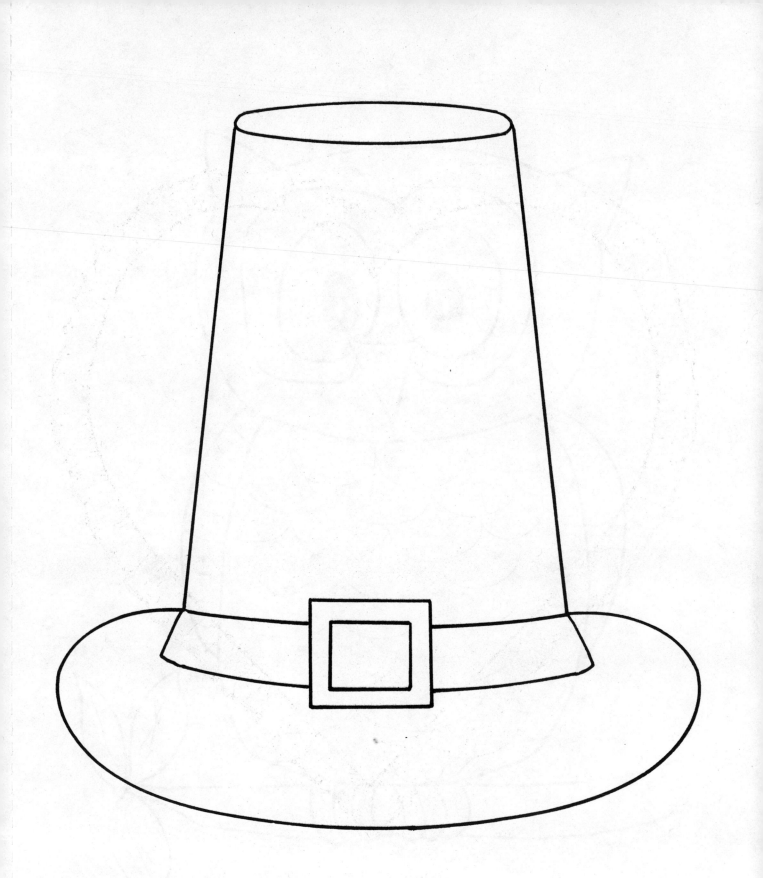

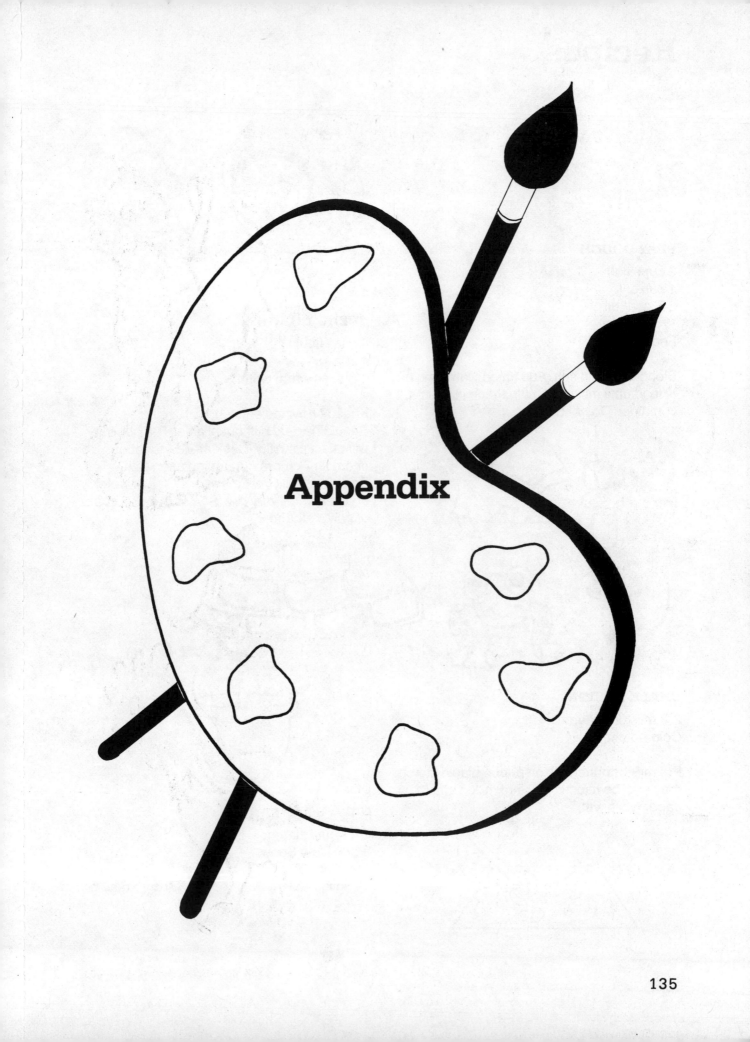

**Appendix**

# Recipes

## PLAY DOUGH

2 cups flour
1 cup salt
2 T. corn oil
½ cup water
Food coloring

Blend flour and salt. Add tinted water and oil. Knead until mixture is stiff. Place in airtight container. Do not bake.

## BREAD DOUGH

4 cups flour
1 cup salt
1½ cups warm water

Knead all ingredients about 10 minutes. Should be very stiff but pliable. The humidity will affect pliability. Cook at 325° for about one hour or more depending upon size. Brush with egg yolk mixed with 1 T. of water and bake until *very dry.* Seal with 2 or 3 coats of polyurethane.

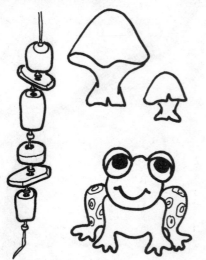

## CHALK DESIGN

2 T. milk or buttermilk
Colored chalk

Put milk or buttermilk on paper. Liquid starch may also be used in place of milk. Chalk paper while wet.

## 3-D or SOAP PAINT

6 T. liquid starch
1 cup Ivory Snow

Whip ingredients with beater. Mixture may be tinted with tempera.

## FINGERPAINT

1 T. boric acid
2 cups flour
1 cup sugar
1 cup cornstarch
2 cups water
Powdered tempera

Mix together flour, sugar, and cornstarch. Add gradually to boiling water. Cook and stir until thick. If too thick add boiling water. Remove and add 1 T. boric acid. Divide and add powdered tempera.

## SQUEEZE PAINT

1 cup liquid starch
1 T. powdered tempera

Mix together and put into a squeeze bottle. Child squeezes the paint onto the paper moving container over paper to form a design.

## SALT PAINT

Mix:  1/3 cup flour
        1/3 cup salt
Add:  Water as desired; different amounts for varied effects. A thin mixture makes puddles and a thicker mixture will sparkle in mounds when dry.
Paint:  On newsprint using large 1/2- to 1-inch brushes.

## BOILED PASTE

Add cold water to 1/2 cup of flour until thick as cream. Simmer and stir on stove for 5 minutes. Store in refrigerator in air tight jar.

## SALT FLOUR DOUGH

Mix 1 cup salt, 3 cups flour, 2 T. cooking oil and enough water to make a soft dough (about ¾ cup). Add vegetable coloring or powdered paint. Store in plastic bag in refrigerator.

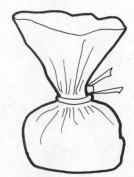

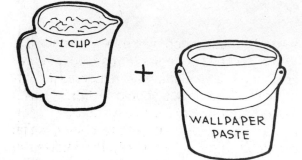

## SAWDUST MODELING MIXTURE

Mix 1 cup of sawdust and ½ cup of wallpaper paste. Add enough water to make mixture like soft putty.

## PASTE JEWELRY MIXTURE

Mix ¾ cup flour, ½ cup cornstarch and ½ cup salt. Add warm water gradually until mixture can be kneaded to reduce stickiness. Mixture may be rolled into balls for beads. Pierce each bead with toothpick or large needle and allow to dry. Paint.

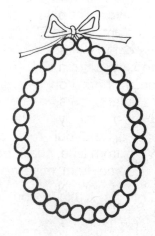

## PAPIER MACHÉ

1. Mix equal parts liquid starch and water. Stir until starch is dissolved. Soak newspaper strips in liquid mixture and pat into place.

2. Combine wallpaper paste (wheat paste) with water to form a fluid paste. Dip paper into mixture and pat into place. (Add powder to water.)

# A Lesson In Color

Color is something that people all over the world enjoy regardless of their nationality or age. We all enjoy watching the beautiful colors in the sunset, a rainbow after a rainstorm, the rippling water of a stream, the blue ocean and crashing waves, the gay colors of a bird, or the delicate petals of a wildflower. Color surrounds us day in and day out whether we are sleeping or awake. Color makes us feel alive, full of energy, peaceful, tired, sad, angry, or happy.

Where are the colors used in our clothing and fabrics, color for paint and crayons made? Most colors are made of pigments or dyes. In the early times, people got their pigments and dyes from natural materials such as insects, bark from trees, and clay. Many plants, plant roots, and leaves provided color too. Today colors such as browns, yellows, and dull reds can come from clay. White from lime, chalk, or gypsum. Some colors come from minerals such as copper, lead and iron. Nature provides us with many pigments, but chemical companies can now produce pigments in large quantities inexpensively.

In order to understand color, one should know how colors are mixed to form new colors. We have included a color wheel with the colors written on the edge in the Appendix. As mentioned previously, you may duplicate a copy for each child and have them add the proper colors or use the color wheel to keep on the bulletin board in the art center. If you choose to keep the color wheel in the art center, you should fill in the sections with colored paper, paint, or crayons. Triangles are provided to show you how to find color triads and near complementary colors. The arrow is used for complementary colors.

The entire list of color terms would be difficult for many elementary students to understand. The basics should be taught to the students, such as primary colors, complementary colors, secondary colors, warm colors, and cool colors. It might be interesting to pick a project out of the book for the class using complementary colors such as red and green, yellow and violet, or blue and orange. Provide a project for the primary colors, one for warm colors, and one for cool colors.

## Color Terms
1. *Primary Colors*—Yellow, red, and blue. These colors are used to make other colors.
2. *Secondary Colors*—The colors that are made when you mix two primary colors. Yellow and blue make green. Yellow and red make orange. Blue and red make violet.
3. *Warm Colors*—The colors on the right side of the color wheel. They remind you of fire and sunlight.
4. *Cool Colors*—The colors on the left side of the color wheel. The colors in nature.
5. *Color Triads*—These colors form a triangle on the color wheel and harmonize. Yellow, blue, and red make a color triad.
6. *Shade*—A shade is darker than the natural color. Red is a natural color and maroon is a shade of red.
7. *Tint*—A tint is lighter than the natural color. Red is a natural color and rose is a tint of red.

*From* The Art Corner © 1979 Goodyear Publishing Company, Inc., *Bonnie Flint Striebel, and Ruth Beazell Forgan*

8. *Adjacent Colors*—Colors that lie next to each other on the color wheel. Yellow and yellow orange are adjacent colors.
9. *Hue*—This word is used to describe the colors red, orange, yellow, green, blue, and violet which are the primary and secondary colors.
10. *High Value*—This is the lightness of a color.
11. *Low Value*—This is the darkness of a color.
12. *Chroma*—This is the lack of grayness. If you mixed blue and gray in different steps, you would have a series of chroma or a chroma chart.

# Color
# Wheel

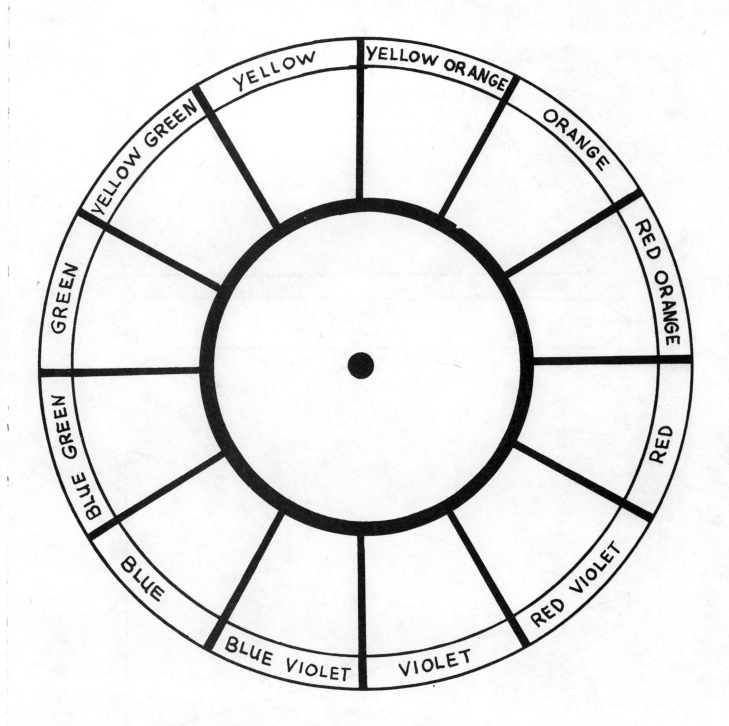

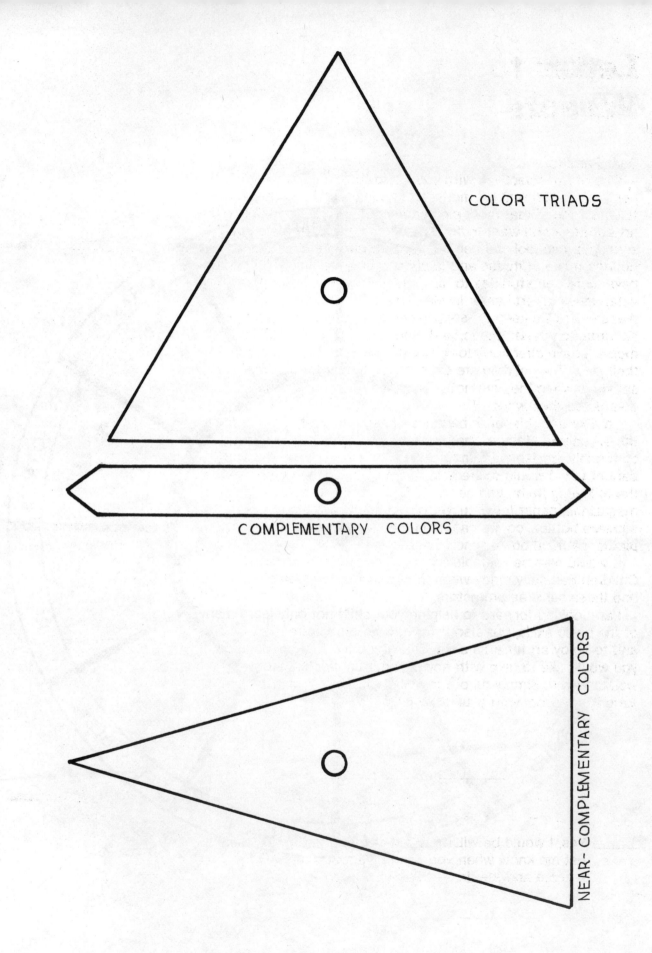

COLOR TRIADS

COMPLEMENTARY COLORS

NEAR-COMPLEMENTARY COLORS

# Letter to Parents

Dear Parents,

One of my objectives with your child this year is to help him or her explore different art media and nourish his or her creative talents. I found that most elementary school children really enjoy art activities and want to "make and do" many art projects. My elementary school children are very creative and I would like to nourish these attitudes and talents. In order to help the children have more opportunities to have art during the school year I have established an art center in the classroom. The art center is a place where we keep art supplies such as paint, scissors, glue, construction paper, fabric, and other art media. Along with the media, I have directions for children to make simple projects on their own. The children are encouraged to use the art center activities when they are not with me or when they have completed their work.

I am writing this letter because I need additional materials for the art center. Many of the items we need are ones that are commonly available around your house and yet ones that we cannot buy. I would appreciate it if you would be willing to save the following items and send them to school with your child: magazines, paper towel tubes, old wallpaper, fabric scraps, squeeze bottles, coffee cans, margarine containers, yarn, paper plates, oatmeal boxes, and newspapers.

It would also be valuable for your child to have an art shirt. Children generally enjoy wearing one of Mom or Dad's old shirts and these serve as protectors.

I am looking forward to helping your child not only learn many of the basic skills, but also learn how to use different art media and to enjoy art for art's sake. Thank you for your cooperation. If you would like to help with any of the art projects, I would welcome you. Simply fill out the bottom half of this letter and send it to school with your child.

Sincerely,

_____
(Teacher's Name)


_____ Yes, I would be willing to aid children during art lessons. Let me know when you can talk about materials I might prepare and the time of the activity.


_____
(Signature)

From The Art Corner © 1979 Goodyear Publishing Company, Inc., Bonnie Flint Striebel, and Ruth Beazell Forgan

# Bulletin
# Board
# Poems

*September*

The freedom of summer has come to an end,
Books and learning should also be friends.
Listen to your teacher, give her your best,
And you'll see how easy to pass a test.

*October*

In fourteen hundred ninety two,
Columbus sailed the ocean blue.
In this month what can you do?
Dress up, go out, and say boo!

*November*

Thanksgiving, turkey, and pumpkin pie,
Arrive in the month of November.
Let's be good citizens, you and I,
So get out and vote, please remember.

*December*

This is my favorite month of the year.
For with it comes the giving of cheer.
If you aren't good, it may appear,
You will get nothing from what I hear!

*January*

The new year begins with a month that is cold.
With icicles, snow, and winds that will blow.
If you live down south you'd have to be told.
For you'd have oranges and grapefruit to hold.

*February*

Hearts and flowers and Valentine fun,
Plus a birthday for Abe and George Washington.

*March*

The March wind will blow
Kites high in the air.
You'll find shamrocks and leprechauns
If you dare!

*April*

April showers bring the flowers of May
But don't forget to play tricks on April Fool's Day!

*May*

Baskets of flowers on the first day of May
And don't forget Mom on her special day.

*June*

Honor your Dad and the flag during June.
Sing "Stars and Stripes Forever"—a catchy tune.

*From The Art Corner © 1979 Goodyear Publishing Company, Inc., Bonnie Flint Striebel, and Ruth Beazell Forgan*

Dear Mom,
We are having an art
project and I need _____
_____ by _____
Thanks _____

Dear Mom,
We are having an art
project and I need _____
_____ by _____
Thanks _____

Dear Mom,
We are having an art
project and I need _____
_____ by _____
Thanks _____

From The Art Corner © 1979 Goodyear Publishing Company, Inc., Bonnie Flint Striebel, and Ruth Beazell Forgan